LIFE AT THE KOP

LIFE AT THE KOP

PHIL NEAL

Macdonald
Queen Anne Press

A Queen Anne Press BOOK

First published in Great Britain in 1986 by
Queen Anne Press, a division of
Macdonald & Co (Publishers) Ltd
Greater London House
Hampstead Road
London NW1 7QX

A BPCC plc Company

British Library Cataloguing in Publication Data

Neal, Phil
Life at the Kop
I. Neal, Phil 2. Soccer players—England—Biography
I. Title
796.334'092'4 GV942.7N3/

ISBN 0-356-12335-9

Photoset in North Wales by
Derek Doyle & Associates, Mold Clywd.
Printed and Bound in Great Britain by
Billing & Sons Ltd., Worcester

ACKNOWLEDGEMENTS

This book could not have been written without the help of David Vear who was responsible for the manuscript or that of Fred Eyre who has injected his own particular brand of humour.

Naturally I should also thank Bob Paisley for dragging me out of football's wilderness, Ian Callaghan for being such an excellent example to me during my early days at Anfield and Ron Greenwood who showed confidence in me when he was England manager.

The contribution of my wife Sue and the rest of the Neal family must not be under-estimated and finally I must thank the fans of Liverpool who for more than a decade inspired me during my life at The Kop.

Contents

1
Liverpool – The End of an Era

I gave Liverpool Football Club the ten best years of my career and what did they give me? They gave me a testimonial, some empty promises and a free transfer. For a decade they held me up as an example to others, a model professional, a thinking footballer and a credit to the game. Then suddenly – overnight almost – I became an embarrassment, yesterday's man with no place in the club's future. The chairman couldn't look me in the eye and the new manager didn't want to play me in the team. Even at a club like Liverpool it's easy to outstay your welcome.

The harsh realities of life as a professional footballer are seldom observed by people outside the game and even on the inside most of us tend to cope by adopting an 'it will never happen to me' attitude. I more than most had reason to live by this philosophy because, after all, I had been promised something. I can remember the words of the club chairman John Smith as clearly now as if they had been spoken yesterday. It was 1982, Liverpool had just regained the League Championship. I was in the England squad for the World Cup finals in Spain and that particular afternoon I was in the chairman's office dotting the 'i's and crossing the 't's on a new four-year contract.

As a player I was still at my peak and well aware of the fact that by signing the contract on offer I would be effectively pledging myself to the club for the rest of my playing days. Other players in a similar position might have had second thoughts – indeed I can think of a number who did. After all I was still in a position to command a substantial transfer fee and, on top of my percentage share from that, I would have had no trouble in negotiating a sweet signing-on fee and a lucrative contract. The exit option was clear in my mind, but on the other hand I was a senior player with the most successful English club in recent history, my family was happy with life on Merseyside and I maintained a naïve belief that loyalty was a quality that would be ultimately rewarded. Naturally I was looking to the future and the only thing I was interested in was remaining in football.

Liverpool is proud of its reputation for promoting from within. The late great Bill Shankly was the last outsider to get the manager's job and he set about creating that famous 'boot-room' team which spawned his successor, Bob Paisley, and then Bob's ultimate successor, Joe Fagan. I wanted to become a part of that same back-room team and the chairman knew it. 'Don't worry Phil, there'll be a job waiting for you here when you finish playing', he told me with a confident, almost paternal, smile. That was all I needed to know and I signed there and then.

Driving home that afternoon I felt sure that the last question-mark over my future had been erased. I was as fit as I'd ever been and was determined to go on playing in the First Division for as long as I could. I'd been lucky with injuries, two compressed fractures of the cheek were the only serious ones worth mentioning, and I was well on the way to setting a club record for consecutive appearances. I remember thinking I'd probably be able to keep the competition at bay for another three seasons before I'd need to think about switching to the coaching staff, but at least the opportunity was there, my loyalty was going to be rewarded.

It never occured to me that the chairman's glib promise was anything less than 100 per cent genuine. As far as I was concerned there was a job available and all the club wanted me to do in the meantime was to maintain my fitness and my form and give them the longest period of service as a player. In reality, the reverse applied because it turned out that the club didn't have the same sort of confidence in my fitness and had expected at best to squeeze a couple more seasons out of me before my legs gave in. The chairman's promise was apparently based on this somewhat mercenary assumption. He thought he'd get every last kick out of me as a player and then offer me a job coaching the club's youngsters for the remainder of my contract. My form and fitness proved to be a graphic illustration of how the best laid plans can go horribly wrong.

The crazy truth is that I was serving the club too well as I pounded up and down the training pitch morning after morning week-in week-out. Publicly my chest swelled with pride as I saw off more and more of my playing contemporaries and privately I would boast about the value for money I was giving through my longevity. Little did I know that far from enhancing my position with the club this dedication to duty would ultimately ensure my departure.

When Joe Fagan emerged from the 'boot-room' to take over from Bob Paisley I was too immersed in playing football to consider the full implications of the move. His elevation created a gap at the bottom of the pile but I hardly gave the matter a second thought when the club announced the appointment of the former Anfield favourite Chris Lawler – known in the game as the 'silent knight' because he seldom opens his mouth and never gets into any bother – as youth team coach. Chris had returned to England after a spell working in Norway and had made it clear that he was looking for a club in the north-west. He just happened to be known and available at the right time. It never occurred to me that his appointment would have a significant bearing on my own future a couple of years later.

Steve Nichol had arrived at the club by this time and was beginning to lay claim to a place in the side. Most people saw him as my successor in the number two shirt but I was determined to make him work for the promotion. I was confident that it would be a few months yet before he had the opportunity to put his size 12s in the skip instead of my size 8s. I felt I was playing as well as ever even though I'd just lost my England place and I was delighted not only to have played, but to have scored two of our goals, in the European Cup final victory over AS Roma in the summer of 1984. The match was won on a dramatic penalty shoot-out, but I scored Liverpool's only real goal of the game as well as a vital penalty after Steve Nichol had put us on the rack by missing his kick.

Even as the 1984-85 season was building towards its climax and I was preparing to lead the side in a second successive European Cup final – this time against Juventus in Brussels – I had no doubts that I would go into the final year of my contract as club captain and first choice right-back. One more season, I was thinking, and then the tracksuit and a whole new future.

1984-85 had been my testimonial year – the traditional chance for the fans to thank a long-serving player for his efforts. Mine had proved a tremendous success thanks to the hard work and dedication of those people organising the seemingly endless stream of functions on my behalf. The supporters had done me proud too: even those to whom I'd never been one of Anfield's brightest stars put their hands in their pockets on my behalf. Such is the spirit of the Merseyside people. The area has considerable problems and the politicians are often quick to criticise, but for me the people of Liverpool are number one. And the city's football fans – even those misguided enough to watch their matches at Goodison Park – are the most knowledgeable and fair-minded in the game.

Football and Liverpool's three-pronged assault on the major titles dominated the days that year and testimonial functions took up every spare evening. Call me naïve if you like, but the internal manoeuvres which, as it turned out, could have stretched the expertise of a scriptwriter from *Dallas*, passed completely over my head.

Joe Fagan, to my knowledge, gave no hints that he was a reluctant boss. Of course, he was 62 years old and in any other job could have been forgiven for thinking that it might be time to swap his football boots for carpet slippers. But although running the playing side of the nation's most successful club is without doubt one of the most demanding jobs in the game, he gave no outward indication that it was proving too much for him. As far as I could see he was coping admirably. He had steered us to a League Championship and European Cup double and while he was too old to hope to beat the record of Bob Paisley, it looked to most of us as if he would carry on for a good while yet. I say most of us because it has become clear as events have unfolded that there were a privileged few at Anfield who knew a good deal more about the situation than the rest of us. Yours truly, even though I was the club captain, was never aware of the existence of a dressing-room cabinet already planning the club's future after Joe's abdication.

I have to laugh when I read editorials on the sports pages of some of the national newspapers and they refer to Liverpool's directors as the 'perfect board'. The stories are generally in response to some highly publicised boardroom row at another club and the writer will cite Liverpool as the outstanding example of a club where directors are seen on match days, provide the money to keep the club on a firm financial footing but are never heard. To the majority of football fans, John Smith is a chairman who knows exactly what the role of a director should be. The Anfield record is there for all to see and everyone considers it a testimony to the chairman's apparent philosophy that directors should stay clear of the dressing-room and leave managing the club to the people who understand the game best.

Let me knock this idea on the head once and for all, because nothing could be further from the truth. John Smith runs Liverpool Football Club 24 hours a day and he exercises an influence over everything from the signing of players down to the wattage of the light bulbs in the club offices. I have no knowledge of his relationship with the abrasive Mr Shankly, but I do know that he was a self-imposed influence on the playing side of the club's activities throughout the reign of Bob Paisley. The record shows Paisley to have been the most successful manager in the history of the British game but few people know that on occasions he was not allowed to make up his own mind on matters as fundamental to the club as which player to sign.

Take the case of Frank McGarvey, a striker who was attracting rave notices at Celtic. The papers were full of speculation about his future and all the top clubs were reported to have been watching him, Liverpool included. Geoff Twentyman, the chief scout, had been to look and couldn't make his mind up. He could see that McGarvey had ability but he wasn't convinced that the lad was any better than a handful of players already with the club. He suggested that Bob should take a look for himself and the manager was of the same mind. He thought that Frank would find it difficult to force his way into the first team. There seemed little doubt that the player had the potential to make it in England, but Bob felt his chances might be limited at Anfield and wasn't prepared to take a gamble, particularly in view of the amount of money that would be involved.

Now there are two local radio stations in Liverpool and one enjoys a far closer relationship with the club than the other, so much so that an excited John Smith felt able to ring one of the lads I know there and to tell him that the club had bought Frank McGarvey for £300,000. 'Great,' said my mate, 'we'll put it out straight away.' 'No,' said the chairman, 'you'd better give me an hour – I haven't told the manager yet!'

Frank McGarvey had a miserable time at Liverpool. From the moment he stepped off the train he must have realised that he wasn't going to enjoy the sort of star treatment he come to expect north of the border. As we already knew, there were too many good players at the club battling for too few places and Frank never made the breakthrough. In the press, his failure was attributed to homesickness and a loss of form but in reality he was a classic victim of Mr Smith's subversive power politics. The chairman had been reading the newspapers and knew that Manchester United, Spurs and Arsenal were heading the list of interested clubs and instead of backing the judgement of his manager, he couldn't bear the thought of losing out to the opposition. From that moment on he would have paid a king's ransom for the player – regardless of the implications for the boy's career – just to stop anyone else from signing him.

Eventually Frank went back to Celtic, never having made a first team appearance for Liverpool, and judging by the reports from Scotland he's playing well and scoring his fair share of goals again. That's not really the point, though, because who's to say he would not have made an impact in England had he been given the opportunity to join another top club with a genuine need for a player with his qualities. Frank got a raw deal, make no mistake about it, but he was lucky compared with another player who'll end up saddled with the label 'Britain's most expensive teenager' for more seasons than he will care to remember.

Again the architect of the headlines is the anonymous Mr Smith but this time the fall guy is Joe Fagan. The player concerned is the 'teenage sensation' Wayne Harrison and the man executing the sting Liverpool's former Merseyside rival Joe Royle – Everton striker turned Oldham Athletic manager. Wayne had made just three first team appearances at Oldham when the carefully fed lines began to crop up in the regional press: 'Great Prospect', 'Rare Talent', 'Star of the Future'. All the usual clichés were wheeled out and of course after a time the scouts took the bait. Geoff Twentyman had a look and to be fair was impressed with the youngster. He thought him an outstanding prospect and recommended that the manager should put a bid in. His general idea was that if the club had £50,000 to spare before the taxman took his cut then it may as well be invested in this particular part of the Futures Market.

Geoff's assessment was a reasonable one but it failed to take into account the extent to which the football grapevine penetrates the boardrooms of Britain's leading clubs. One evening each week Joe Royle can be found down at The Cliff – Manchester United's training ground – playing five-a-side with a group of former pros including the United manager, Ron Atkinson. One particular week he must have mentioned the promise of young Wayne Harrison and Ron obviously expressed some passing interest. Within days he was a Liverpool player – signed on the chairman's orders for a staggering £250,000 after playing just five times for Oldham's first team. Mr Smith was prepared to pay five times the youngster's worth rather than see a teenage prospect join our arch-rivals United.

So far Wayne has never threatened to break through into the first team. He's young, raw and has an awful lot to learn. At Boundary Park he used to go to work on the bus whereas now he drives a big BMW, but that's about the only thing that has changed. To me, Wayne looks like a bewildered youngster who has just been taken away from his friends and cannot for the life of him work out why. At this stage I would say it is touch and go whether he will ever make the grade yet if he fails at Liverpool and moves elsewhere, wherever he goes he will have to live with the implications of that six-figure price tag and all the pressure that goes with it. Such is the chairman's influence over the daily life of the football club.

In the spring of 1985 Mr Smith was facing up to the fact that Joe Fagan had been a wrong choice as manager. He had maintained the continuity after Bob Paisley's retirement but had neither the stamina nor the inclination to make the necessary commitment in the long term. Unbeknownst to me, Joe had spent long sessions with the chairman discussing the options for the future and had eventually decided to retire at the end of the season, giving the chairman a few months' breathing-space in which to find a successor. Just one other person was in on the secret.

Kenny Dalglish, just a month younger than me and fighting a long-term battle with injury, was also apparently thinking about his future now that his contract was running out. He'd never given any indication that he harboured managerial ambitions and most people expected him to finish his playing days at Anfield and then slip back to Scotland where his family has a substantial business interest. For several seasons Kenny's state of fitness had been one of Anfield's most closely guarded secrets. He would train only on a Thursday – traditionally one of the lightest work days of the week – and spent the remainder of his time either on the treatment table or resting. He was never asked to take part in the gruelling 'shuttles', the sprinting and turning exercises that are the bane of a footballer's life, and the most strenuous activities he took part in were the leisurely five-a-sides. I often wondered how he stood up to the pace of First Division football and came to the conclusion that he survived because he was exposed only in short bursts around the penalty box. Had he been a busy sort of player – committed for 90 minutes of every game – I'm sure he would have been forced to step down some time before.

To the fans Kenny was an idol, probably more popular even than Kevin Keegan had been. Off the field, though, he was a quiet, complex sort of character who kept himself to himself and spent most of his afternoons resting in bed. No one could really claim to know him well and so none of us had any knowledge of where his true ambitions lay, none of us that is except the chairman!

The story broke at the worst possible time for all of us, on the eve of the European Cup final. Joe was shattered that the news of his impending retirement had been leaked in advance of such an important game and I was staggered that it had been Kenny's name had been floated in the press as the certain successor. At first I was inclined to dismiss the notion as newspaper speculation, but when Kenny refused to be drawn on the subject and the chairman was careful to avoid dismissing the idea things began to look ominous. I'd never even considered the idea of switching straight from playing to managing the club. Naturally I saw myself as Joe's successor but was convinced he would stay on for a couple more seasons to enable me to serve some sort of apprenticeship. It wasn't that I didn't feel capable of doing the job, more that it seemed inconceivable that a club as conservative as Liverpool would take this sort of gamble.

Kenny's appointment as player-manager was confirmed when we arrived back from Belgium. The shock of the Brussels massacre had numbed the squad and the future was the last thing on our minds as we touched down at Speke Airport. Gradually, though, I was forced to face up to the grim fact that the nightmare I was living through was real. It was the most devastating week of my life. In the space of five days, the dreams and ambitions I had striven for over a decade had been shattered. Realistically, I could never now hope to manage Liverpool and a huge question-mark was hanging over my future at the club.

The season had ended in the most calamitous fashion and the club officials were fighting for Liverpool's European life. Even the press had accepted the shock news of Kenny's elevation to manager in a relatively low key fashion – such was the impact of the Heysel Stadium disaster.

There was no one around to talk to, no one to offer me advice about the future, I was well and truly out on my own. I retreated into myself and for my wife Sue and our children Ashley and Natasha life must have been very difficult. I refused to talk to anyone – I seemed to have lost the ability to communicate – and if the phone rang I would insist that Sue answered it no matter how difficult it might have been for her to do so. I spent hours in the garden of our home on the outskirts of Liverpool. We'd bought it only a couple of years earlier with the future in mind. We both loved the district and it was our dream home. Neither of us wanted to leave but now I was being forced to face up to that prospect.

Later I took the family to our holiday retreat in Scotland in yet another effort to get away from it all and get my thoughts into some sort of order. I did some walking and played a bit of golf but it didn't help, and matters were made worse by the fact that Sue, who had been unwell for some time, had been told by doctors that she needed a major operation. Life for the Neal family was progressing under a huge, dark cloud.

Back home it was time to prepare for the new season and for the first time in my career I was dreading the prospect. Driving to the ground the first morning I remember thinking about Kenny and vowing to myself that I would never call him 'boss'. Silly now, I know, but at the time it was psychologically very important to me to maintain some independence. Outwardly – as club captain – I knew it was my duty to put on a dignified brave face, but inwardly my mind was in turmoil. The Brussels massacre and the club's subsequent ban from European competition had cast a shadow over life at Anfield. Most of the lads were very subdued and all were apprehensive about the prospect of working with Kenny in his new role because no one had any idea about just how he was proposing to play things.

Training remained in the hands of Ronnie Moran and Roy Evans so that meant a familiar routine and I threw myself into it as hard as I had ever done previously. I neither expected nor received any favours and I knew that I could not expect to be an automatic choice in the side. I knew I had no future at Liverpool but I was equally determined that I would not give up my number two shirt without one hell of a fight. The club's European commitments the previous season had resulted in my testimonial game with Everton being held over. It had been rescheduled for a date just weeks into the new season and the last thing I wanted was to be summoned back from the reserves for my big night.

In the event I was in the side when we opened the season at home to Arsenal, but there was an uneasy feeling around. The newspaper speculation about my future had gathered momentum and there was talk of me moving to Oxford United as player-coach. I did receive a telephone call, in fact, but it came in the weeks leading up to my testimonial match so I decided to delay any negotiations until that was out of the way. In the event they never came back to me so I can only assume they either had second thoughts or found someone else.

My testimonial night turned out to be a tremendous success, the fans responded and everyone connected with the project played their part to make sure things went like clockwork. Even Sue, who by this time had had her operation and was back home convalescing, managed to attend. I think it was the only time I was genuinely able to put my problems to one side and enjoy the occasion. The next day was a real anti-climax because for more than a year the testimonial had taken up the majority of my time. The fact that it was now over and I had only my future survival to concern myself with deflated me still further. I decided that I would have to get my act together for everyone's sake so I requested a meeting with the chairman. In my heart of hearts I knew that there was only one way the meeting could go but nevertheless I wanted to hear him speak the words that would seal my fate.

The face said it all as I entered his office, unlike at our meeting three years earlier there was no need for him to be reassuring. I felt like one of the hundreds of petty criminals who have appeared before him at the Liverpool magistrates court. I was waiting for his verdict on my future. His answer left little room for discussion – there wasn't one! Sure, I'd served the club well and that had been rewarded with my testimonial, but as far as the promise of a job was concerned Mr Smith seemed to have had an attack of amnesia. Of course he agreed that it would have been nice for me to have continued to serve the club but I was in the wrong place at the wrong time and there wasn't a job for me. Naturally the club wouldn't stand in my way if I felt a move was in my best interests and that was the end of the meeting. As in 1982 the discussion was brought to a close with a smile, only this time it was condescending and the chairman's eyes were riveted on the wall to the side of me.

I closed the door behind me and suddenly remembered an event some years ago involving one the Anfield greats, John Toshack. He'd gone off to Swansea to serve what he believed to be his managerial apprenticeship prior to taking over the Liverpool job when Bob Paisley retired. He, too, had been given the nod by Mr Smith and was convinced he would be recalled to Merseyside as soon as the time was right. He even paraded before The Kop in a Liverpool shirt when he brought his Swansea side to Anfield for the first time – a clear indication of where his loyalties lay. But when the time came for Bob to call it a day Tosh's phone failed to ring and some people say he has never really recovered from the snub.

The press had got wind of my audience with the chairman and there was a group of reporters waiting when I emerged from the ground. I was angry but I resisted the temptation to shoot my mouth off and instead gave an accurate but toned-down version of events tailing off with the statement that it had been made clear by the club, for its own reasons, that there wasn't a long-term future for me there and that I was free to consider alternative offers.

Mild enough comments under the circumstances – but the next day I was stripped of the club captaincy!

Kenny called me into his office and told me he was giving the job to Alan Hansen because of what I had said in the press. I felt justifiably aggrieved, but the news merely served to focus my mind and I decided that I must get away from Anfield as soon as possible.

The final straw came a week later at West Ham. The side didn't play well and we lost the game 2-1. The lads were arguing among themselves as we got back into the dressing-room but it was nothing too serious. Then right out of the blue, Ronnie Moran spun round on me and snapped: 'Well, its all right for you Nealy, you've had all you want!'. It was an indirect reference to my testimonial and although it was voiced in the heat of the moment it cut me to the bone. I'd sweated blood for the club over a decade and this was my thanks … I couldn't believe what I was hearing!

I kept my cool with difficulty but the weekend did nothing to temper my outrage and the following Monday I pulled the coach to one side and told him exactly what I thought. Naturally he apologised but the sentiment stuck with me and I began wondering whether I was being used as some sort of scapegoat for the team's early season problems.

By the time the derby with Everton came around in September Kenny had relegated me to the substitute's bench and the writing was well and truly on the wall. Ironically I came on as substitute in midfield and played a blinder but it made no difference, there was no way I was going to play myself back into the team.

When David Booth resigned as manager of Second Division Grimsby Town there was speculation in the newspapers that I would be taking over. I'd made it plain that I was prepared to discuss offers and when their chairman, Mr Middleton, contacted me I said I was interested. After all, both Bill Shankly and Lawrie

McMenemy had served their managerial apprenticeships at Blundell Park, so I would be in good company. David had done a brilliant job at Grimsby, transforming the side from a mediocre Third Division outfit into a club hovering in the Second Division promotion zone and, according to their chairman, harbouring First Division ambitions.

From the word go, though, I had nagging self-doubts. David was leaving to join a family business in Tenerife because, he said, the club had achieved all that it could under his stewardship. Call me cynical if you like, but I interpreted that as a euphemism for a situation in which the club had finally fulfilled its natural potential and wasn't geared up for Division One. What is more I'd phoned a few contacts who had all warned me that the Blundell Park boardroom was a snake-pit. I wasn't in awe of the challenge, I just thought I had a right to know the ground rules before I decided to play the game.

I went across to Humberside to meet the directors and, to be fair, Mr Middleton was brilliant. I asked him about the boardroom squabbles and he didn't try to duck the issue. Yes, there had been problems, but everything had been sorted out and there was optimism about the future. I have to admit I was tempted for a moment and at that point, particularly with things having gone sour at Liverpool, I was wavering. Remember, at Anfield I was being treated like a spare p ... at a wedding now that Kenny had given me the elbow.

The next step was to take the family across for a look at what might possibly become our new home. Kenny was delighted to excuse me a day's training – by that time I'd been left out of the first team altogether and the manager hadn't suggested I should go into the reserves. The irony is that I was feeling desperately short of match practice and would have welcomed a game in the youth team if I could have passed the referee's pre-match inspection!

However, there we were on Humberside. I was playing the cheerful father: 'I'll have this lot in the First Division within a year, Ashley'. Sue was being the supportive wife and mother: 'Don't worry, Natasha, there are plenty of open spaces for riding'.

At the same time I was thinking: 'Christ, I'm going to have to drive miles to see a match and David Booth must have had the charisma of Tommy Docherty to persuade players to come here'. Sue was thinking: 'I've got to find us a home here and what's this funny smell?'. Natasha was thinking: 'Do they still use horses and carts?', and Ashley wanted to know: 'How will you get me back to Merseyside for training with the lads at Formby?'.

The final decision was an agonising one. I knew I would be stretching family loyalty to the limit if I took the job and at the same time my friends were advising me not to be hasty. With your confidence eroded it's easy to jump at the first job that is offered and when all is said and done, Grimsby Town may be an unfashionable club but it has proved the springboard for some pretty outstanding managerial careers. When I finally said 'no' it was one of the hardest decisions I had ever had to make. The lads at Liverpool were surprised, but I'm not sure that Kenny was because although we hadn't been on the best of terms over the preceding few weeks, he did take the trouble to pull me to one side at the time of the Grimsby offer and to advise me to take my time, and to think of the family before accepting any offer. Nevertheless, I wonder what Mr Smith was thinking as I decided – for the time being – to remain on the Anfield payroll?

I developed a sixth sense about the future and became convinced that the break I was looking for was just around the corner. Football is an unforgiving game and there is no room for sentiment, a fact I was learning the hard way. Consequently it came as no surprise when the first casualties of the 1985-86 season began to fall.

The newspapers linked me with Burnley – I was never contacted. And Preston – climbing Everest paled alongside that challenge! Then Bolton – 'sleeping giants'! I'd heard the cliché a dozen times before, usually used by directors or incoming managers to win over the hard core fans of previously successful clubs, so why should Bolton be any different?

Strangely, one of the things that attracted me to Burnden Park was the fact that there was only one direction in which the club could go and that was up! Bolton had hit rock bottom and the directors knew it. They were broke, although in the process of refloating the company by selling off surplus space for development, and they warned me that I'd have little money to spend. They were asking me to save them from relegation to the Fourth Division yet promising me nothing except a two-and-a-half year contract and the promise that if I saw that out successfully then the money from a multi-million-pound sports and leisure complex would put the club back in the black.

In view of the financial stability of Grimsby Town and their healthy Second Division status there was no contest, but I wanted a challenge and the phrase 'sleeping giants' is a haunting one. I had an hour with the Bolton board on the Tuesday evening and later that night the chairman phoned to offer me the job. I broke the news to Kenny the next day and he was delighted for me.

On the Thursday morning on my way to the news conference at Burnden Park that would announce my appointment I stopped off at Anfield for the last time to collect my belongings. My 12 pairs of boots were lying waiting in a cardboard box in reception, Kenny had taken the morning off and the chairman was presumably punishing another line-up of petty criminals. I may have been in this game for a long time but football never ceases to surprise me.

2

Brussels – Football's Night of Shame

Experienced footballers develop a sort of instinct. It can tell you when the team is in the right frame of mind for victory and, believe me, Liverpool were certainly in the mood as they left Speke Airport to defend their European Cup title against Juventus in Brussels.

For the 'Reds', it hadn't been the most successful end to the 1984-85 season. Manchester United had beaten us after a replay in the semi-finals of the FA Cup and we'd surrendered the League Championship to our Merseyside arch rivals Everton. The final blow had come at Goodison Park a few days before when Howard Kendall's side had beaten us 1-0 in the last game of the competition.

At many clubs, players would have been wanting bonuses for finishing runners-up in the League Championship and reaching the FA Cup semi-finals, but not at Liverpool, this just wasn't our way. As far as we were concerned, our last chance to salvage something from what had been a disappointing season would come in the Heysel Stadium the following night. Retaining the European Cup was all that concerned us.

Liverpool's record of consistency in Europe is unparalleled in British football: four times previously we had won the European Cup and the bookmakers had made us favourites to extend that run to five. Juventus, though, were to provide glamorous opposition, their side studded with a galaxy of stars brought together in Turin at enormous cost.

Only a club backed by the massive Fiat Car Corporation and owned by the multi-millionaire Giovanni Agnelli could afford world-class stars like Platini, Rossi, Tardelli and Boniek. Even so, their side had finished a disappointing fifth in the Italian League championship and so the management was under enormous pressure to succeed. We were under no illusions about the size of the task facing us: I felt the game was likely to be the toughest European Cup challenge we had faced since we first lifted the trophy after a 3-1 victory over Borussia Moënchengladbach on a memorable night in Rome back in May 1977.

Alongside the Italian squad we were largely a team of nobodies. Kenny Dalglish and Ian Rush were, I'm sure, well known to the opposition as a feared strike force, but I'd have been surprised if there were hefty dossiers on the rest of us. Liverpool's success stems from the fact that the team performs like a well-oiled machine. The side has always comprised good players but I always felt that the key to its consistent success lay mostly in the way the management established continuity and then allowed the lads to develop their own understanding.

At 34 I was honest enough to accept that my playing days were numbered and that only made me even more determined to add another European Cup winners' medal to my collection before hanging up my boots. As club captain I had been taking the keenest interest in the way preparations were going and in my view the side was at the peak of its form. Sustain that level of commitment on the night, I thought, and we'll be home and dry. At Liverpool, preparation for foreign games, whether pre-season tournaments or deadly serious European Cup matches, never varied. Always we would train at Melwood on the Monday and then fly out to the venue the day before the fixture. We always chartered a plane from Aer Lingus – the shamrock was apparently a lucky symbol for us – and the spare capacity after the players, the press, and the wives had been accounted for was sold off to supporters in the form of executive travel packages. The arrangement was so successful that the club even turned in a healthy profit on the deal.

A crowd of several hundred had been at Speke to wish us *bon voyage* and warn us in no uncertain terms that we would not be welcomed back with open arms without the trophy. The lads signed the usual, seemingly endless string of autographs and then we finally boarded the jet for the short hop to Belgium. Seat belt unfastened and with Merseyside a patchwork quilt below us as the plane banked and climbed towards the cloud base I found myself drifting back through the years and over one or two of those incidents that give footballers the memories to treasure long after their playing days have been left behind.

For me, Europe would provide many of the memories from my career at Liverpool. For the club player there is no finer stage on which to display his talents and for the club man there is no better way to experience the sort of comradeship that is felt by those lucky enough to become a part of a settled and successful squad. At Liverpool I had experienced so much of both the images in my mind that morning were of so many different things.

I remembered the momentous scale of the Merseyside welcome when we returned triumphant from Rome. My penalty goal had sealed our victory after efforts from Terry McDermott and Tommy Smith, but it was a triumph for the old Liverpool – the squad I had joined less than two years earlier – and I recalled the emotion of players like Ian Callaghan, Emlyn Hughes, Steve Highway and, of course, 'Smithy'. That night belonged to them because they had been a part of Bill Shankly's Liverpool and this was their reward.

Half a million people had turned out to pay homage as we paraded Europe's most coveted club trophy in Liverpool for the first time and in his eagerness to usher us out on to the Town Hall balcony the Lord Mayor completely overlooked the fact that the free-flowing champagne had begun to take its inevitable toll on the bladders of some of the lads. The fans had been waiting for hours for a glimpse of their triumphant heroes and were in no mood to let us take a quick bow. Terry Mac to the side of me was doubled up yet trapped with nowhere to go and in the end the inevitable happened. The unsuspecting St John's Ambulanceman, 50 feet below but directly in the line of fire, must have thought he'd been caught in a freak spring shower because he made no complaints.

One of the more audacious Liverpool press photographers did capture the incident for posterity but thankfully wasn't the type to want to make a quick killing out of the picture. It remained in his 'black album' of unpublished photographs for years and Terry, for his part, was in future always willing to spend those extra few minutes obliging even the most pedantic of lensmen just in case there were one or two copies of the shot in circulation.

The atmosphere on the plane was as relaxed as usual. The players were in the front section sealed off from everyone else and our wives and girlfriends were being looked after towards the centre by the club's sponsors. The plan was to check into the hotel and then train later at the headquarters of Anderlecht, the Belgian league champions. The sun was shining and it was a beautiful spring afternoon as we touched down in the Belgian capital. Another memory from the dim and distant past flooded back to me, but the weather conditions on that occasion couldn't have been further removed from those on this May afternoon.

We'd been drawn against the East German champions Dynamo Dresden and after romping through the first leg 5-1 we were facing the long haul almost to the Polish border for the return. The match was scheduled during the heart of the bitterly cold European winter and I remember looking up the temperatures in the newspapers during the days leading up to the game. Every day the noon temperature was something like -10°C and in the end I was so worried that I went out and bought myself a sheepskin coat. When word got out among the other lads I became the butt of the dressing-room jokes and none were taking the mickey more than Phil Thompson and Terry McDermott. They told me in no uncertain terms that they were hard lads from Kirkby (one of Merseyside's toughest and most deprived districts) and there was no way that they were going soft and wrapping themselves up in overcoats.

I tried to reason with them but it was no good, and on the day we set off they turned up at the airport in tee-shirts. It was cold enough for me in Liverpool, but Terry and Phil were thoroughly enjoying themselves as they settled down for the three-and-a-half hour flight. It was the middle of the afternoon but pitch dark as we came in to land. The cheery Irish pilot switched on the intercom to inform us that there was a blizzard blowing on the ground. Still our hard Kirkby lads didn't get the message. 'Ay Nealy, this snow's gonna ruin your new coat', Thommo shouted, and Terry chipped in: 'Yeh, good job we've come in something washable!'.

The plane taxied to a halt and the steps were wheeled up to the cabin door. As the hostess swung it open a blast of icy air swept down the cabin. Thommo and Terry were on their feet and already making for the exit, keen to show the rest of us that they were made of sterner stuff. 'Come on lads, have you never seen a bit of snow before?' Phil yelled as he disappeared through the hatch, and then seconds, later: 'F... me, where's the f...... bus? You could freeze the f...... b.... off a brass f...... monkey out here!'. Phil Thompson was well known at Anfield for his quick wit and articulate command of the English language. He was the only man I knew who could manage to slip an expletive slap bang in the middle of a word. On this occasion, though, even he was beaten and within seconds both he and Terry were reduced to shivering wrecks and begging for blankets.

Weeks later, a couple of days before the quarter-final tie

with Benfica Phil sidled up to me one lunch-time after training. 'Where did you get your sheepskin from 'cos I'm thinking of getting one for the trip next week'. I couldn't believe what I was hearing but equally I couldn't resist the chance to get my own back so I pointed him in the right direction and told him to mention my name to the manager of the shop to ensure that he would get the best possible treatment. Sure enough, the squad assembled on the eve of the game with 15 of us in lightweight suits – ready for the muggy southern European climate – and Thommo resplendent in his brand new sheepskin. Geography had apparently never been one of his strong points at school!

Safely checked into our Brussels hotel and with our families being looked after separately by the sponsers who had laid on a whole range of activities to keep them amused between our arrival and match time, the squad got down to the serious business of preparing for the match. Traditionally, we always like to have a run-out as soon as possible after arriving at a Continental venue. The thinking is that it enables the players to stretch their legs and work off some of the pre-match tension that inevitably builds up during the idle hours spent flying.

The Anderlecht stadium was first-rate, the facilities excellent and the playing surface in superb condition – psychologically things couldn't have been better. After a warm-up routine we moved into an easy yet energetic practice match. Emlyn Hughes was with us on the trip and he joined in for part of the session. Afterwards he told me that he felt the players were in an ideal frame of mind for the next day's match. He too shared that same instinct, born from his own experience as a player and club captain, and he was convinced we would get the right result. It's quite difficult to pinpoint exactly what those all important signs are, but the competitive edge to the players, the fluid way in which they were stringing together their passes and the general exuberance of their football were all contributory factors. We returned to the hotel happy and relaxed, feeling totally in control of our game and at the same time excited by the knowledge that the countdown to the final had begun.

At Liverpool there have never been any hard and fast rules about when to get up or when to be in bed, what should be allowed and what mustn't be done under any circumstances. In all my years at the club I never saw the Football League's codebook for players' behaviour ... it just wasn't part of the Anfield way. The fact that we were in Brussels on the eve of the European Cup final was considered no more special – in terms of preparation – than any First Division match back home. Some of the lads were in bed early, a part of their own pre-match routine, others preferred to stay up a little later and relax in the hotel lounges. The game wasn't scheduled to kick off until the following evening so there would be plenty of time to rest up.

As usual there were plenty of sports journalists milling around the players, some welcome, some not so. One or two of the players joined the groups of reporters from time to time but generally they were gossiping rather than handing out any state secrets from the Liverpool camp. Little did I know at the time, but the biggest and best kept secret in Anfield's history had already been filed by telephone to London in good time to make sensational headlines in the following day's national papers. From a reporter's point of view the timing couldn't have been better ... the most sensational Liverpool story since Kevin Keegan announced he was going to quit the club for Hamburg, but with even more poignant timing. As for Kevin, we had all known that he would be leaving us after the Rome final and the fact served to motivate us still further to ensure that he would go out on a high. This time, though, the story was disturbing in that it created an atmosphere of uncertainty. The fact that it first appeared on the very day of the game proved a serious threat to our concentration.

Craig Johnston was one of the first to get hold of the newspaper on the morning of the game and he apparently bumped into my wife and Mark Lawrenson's girlfriend, who had decided to duck out of the obligatory tour of the sights of the Belgian capital. Sue told me later that she had been staggered to hear that Joe had decided to retire but had laughed with disbelief at Craig's revelation that press speculation linked Kenny with the job. Like me, she had never considered him to be even remotely interested and had always felt that he would return to Scotland once his playing days were over. She was so dismissive of Craig's tale that she never thought any more about the matter until she bumped into Kenny's wife, Marina, about half an hour later.

Sue was puzzled that Marina had also made her excuses and not gone sight-seeing, but when she asked why Marina was non-committal, almost evasive. Clearly the truth was beginning to dawn, but Sue neither believed the story nor fully understood the implications for the two of us and our family. The rumour spread like wildfire through the team hotel and the atmosphere was chaotic – never before had I experienced such scenes in the hours leading up to a match. The reporters were clamouring for a statement and individual players were being hounded for 'inside information'. In the end Joe made a statement, but it served only to fuel the rumours rather than to either confirm or scotch them. By saying he regretted that the story had leaked out and that there would be no further statement until after the European Cup final he merely – in journalistic terms – lent the story credibility.

But how had the story got out? I genuinely believe that Joe was shattered when he saw the newspapers on the morning of the game, so I cannot believe that he had let anything slip. Kenny, for his part, had always been his own man and I cannot ever remember him forging a particularly close relationship with any one sports journalist, yet somehow the story had been revealed to just one man and his article was so close to the mark that his information could only have come from inside the club. I spent half an hour in my room trying to think things over.

Trying to separate fact from fantasy can be difficult at the best of times and it was the last thing I should have been doing in the hours leading up to a match which had promised to be the climax of my career. Fortunately, my sense of professionalism is something that I have prided myself on throughout my career, and although this was indeed its biggest test, I did manage to regain some sort of control. I was in Brussels to lead Liverpool to a fifth European Cup victory, I told myself, and I was proud to be captaining the side. I must lead by example and shut this news and its implications out of my mind until we are back in Liverpool, I was arguing to myself, and gradually I regained my composure. If Joe was retiring, and all the signs pointed to the fact that he was, then I reasoned that I did have a claim to the crown. If the directors had already made up their minds about a successor then surely they would have put an end to this unsettling speculation by naming him. The fact that they hadn't indicated to me that they might not have finally made up their minds.

No, I told myself, you're still in the frame, Phil, and you can do yourself a lot of good by playing a captain's game tonight. Return to Liverpool leading a team of footballing heroes and then start staking your claim for the manager's chair. Who could fault the strategy? Results are all that matter in football and only after the right result has been achieved should the talking begin. I had collected my thoughts and was emerging from my room the captain of Liverpool and more determined than ever to keep my hands on that European trophy.

Thankfully the positive atmosphere of the previous day had returned by the time we left for the Heysel Stadium and the boys were ready to go to work. As usual we left in good time for the short drive to the ground but already the streets were thronged with fans. Both sets of supporters had converged on the city in the hours leading up to the game and all roads now led to the ground. Two hours before the kick-off we were taking our first look at the cavernous dressing-room below the main stand. It's strange, I know, in the light of what subsequently happened, but my first impression of that stadium was the sheer size of the dressing-room and my second the generally down-at-heel appearance of the place. Four times I had appeared in the European Cup final, twice in Rome, once in Paris and of course at Wembley – this place was certainly a poor relation.

All of us wanted to get a glimpse of the pitch and some measure of the atmosphere so we decided to go out on to the field. Access was by means of half-a-dozen steps and as we emerged into the evening sunshine there was a junior curtain-raiser game going on. Even so, long before the kick-off, the ground was filling up and we could see a large contingent of Liverpool fans towards the bottom corner of the field. Naturally the lads wandered down towards them. We had always considered the support of the Liverpool fans a vital element in our success on the field. Tonight, against Juventus – a side followed with an all-consuming passion rivalled in Britain only by the supporters of Celtic, Rangers or Manchester United – we knew we would need all the help we could get.

The atmosphere among the fans in that bottom corner of the ground was relaxed and good-natured. 'Liv-er-pool, Liv-er-pool', greeted us from the moment our figures, clad specially for the occasion in new club suits, emerged from the tunnel. There was only one direction in which to go and as we reached the enclosure, the lads were waving to the fans and the supporters were throwing good luck tokens in our direction. A plastic football bounced in front of us and Craig chipped it back into the crowd. Seconds later it was back, this time at the feet of Sammy Lee, and he juggled it about before flicking it back. When the ball came back out a third time Bruce did a trick or two. The atmosphere at that time was tremendous, no tension whatsoever and the players – naturally wound up with the prospect of such an important game ahead of them – were grateful for the diversion.

A substantial contingent of Juventus fans were also filing into the ground and their enclosure was separated from the Liverpool one by a wire fence. I remember thinking at the time that the two groups of supporters were very close and how such an arrangement would never be sanctioned in Britain. I was also struck at the time by the absence in substantial numbers of policemen, but assumed that they must be due to arrive at any moment.

With an hour to go before the kick-off we retreated to the sanctuary of our dressing-room to begin preparing for the game. As usual on such a big occasion, the business area of the stadium was bustling with people, many connected with the two clubs, dozens associated with the European governing body, UEFA, and those few privileged hangers-on who always seem to get passes for the inner sanctum. The prospect of a final between two such evenly-matched teams had generated considerable interest and the organisers were anticipating a capacity crowd. One thing that sticks in my mind is the memory of the noise from the rival fans as the minutes began ticking away.

As usual in the Liverpool dressing-room preparation was left largely to the individual and although I was going about my business quietly in one corner of the room, setting myself up mentally for the challenge ahead, one or two of the other players – particularly those lads not actually in the team on the night – kept nipping outside the door and up the steps leading to the pitch to take in the atmosphere. I still don't really know when the good-natured rivalry that we had witnessed earlier turned into hostile baiting but I remember hearing one of the lads report that some fighting had broken out on that same far terrace we had been saluting earlier. Sadly, fighting has become a common sight on football terraces not only in

Britain but in many parts of Europe too, and so I didn't show any particular interest in what was happening at first. My mind was focused on the match ahead. The police presence remained pathetically inadequate and even as the fighting worsened and the rival mobs began bombarding each other with missiles there were no signs of reinforcements being drafted in.

The collapse of the terrace wall which brought about the carnage and resulted in the loss of 38 lives could be heard clearly in our dressing-room – a dull but sickening thud half-masked by the noise from the rest of the rapidly-filling stadium. Craig and a couple of the other players poked their heads out of the tunnel mouth to see what was going on and reported back that some people appeared to be injured and that ambulancemen were on the scene. Hundreds of fans had spilled out on to the pitch and were being herded together by the riot police who had, at last, arrived. A few minutes later a harrassed-looking UEFA official put his head round the door and reported that there had been an accident, that a wall had collapsed and that we should be prepared for a delay in the kick-off.

In the corridor outside our dressing-room officials were bustling to and fro in an atmosphere of total confusion. No one was prepared to tell us just what was going on, but at that stage I don't believe the organisers were themselves aware of the scale of the tragedy. Craig, who was down as one of our substitutes on the night, was one of the first players to realise that something was terribly wrong. He came back into the dressing-room and told us that it looked serious. He said he'd seen people being carried away unconscious. A few minutes later he was back telling us that he'd heard someone had died.

From the moment he made that grim announcement, the atmosphere in the dressing-room changed. It was like letting the air out of a balloon slowly. Everyone knew that the situation had now become serious and would inevitably cast a shadow over the game, and immediately the jokes that had helped ease pre-match nerves stopped and heads started to drop. Next came news that five people were dead, but the information was being passed to us unofficially by word of mouth. So far no UEFA official had put his head round our door since the first announcement that the kick-off would be delayed.

Then the full horror began to unfold before our very eyes. The emergency services turned a car park area behind the main stand into a temporary mortuary and from our dressing-room windows, which were high in our wall but at ground level, we could see the stretcher-bearers carrying body after body past us. Incredibly, although everyone in the ground must have been aware that there had been some sort of tragedy, the atmosphere in the stadium remained angry and hostile. Fans from both sides were still rampaging on the very terrace from which the dead and injured were being removed. They were hurling missiles at each other – anything that came to hand from beer cans and wine bottles to lumps of concrete and iron railings. From the mouth of the tunnel I watched in stunned silence as the warring factions fought out their pitched battle.

There still seemed to be far too few police in the stadium and those who were there appeared to have no idea about what they should be doing. Instead of organising their ranks and then moving in between the fighting fans they merely stood in front of the terracing using their riot shields to fend off the many missiles that were being hurled in their direction. Even when a mounted police division was drafted in, the riders chose to gallop up and down the centre of the field rather than to get in and separate the hooligans.

Inside the tunnel chaos reigned. UEFA officials and the referee were meeting with representatives of the two clubs and the man in charge of the police operation in an effort to establish a consensus view of the best way forward. I was staggered by the general hysteria of the UEFA people and the police. It was obvious that neither side was geared up even for an unexpected emergency, never mind the full scale disaster which was unfolding before our very eyes and the battle that was continuing outside. There seemed to be no one willing to take nor indeed capable of taking control of the situation.

Appeals for calm were being broadcast regularly over the stadium's public address system but they were neither heard nor heeded by the mob. There was talk of cancelling the match altogether but I believed this would be the craziest step of all. Had the game been called off I felt the violence would not only have continued but probably escalated and spilled over into the streets of Brussels. In that event there could have been only one outcome ... even more casualties. I knew that the match must go ahead and I was convinced that as long as the riot police surrounded the pitch and faced the crowd, thus protecting the players, then the football would provide a stabilising distraction. It was a gamble, I know, but the alternative was unthinkable.

By this time, though, the death toll had climbed into the 30s and while the police had managed to gain some degree of control, the officials were still arguing about what they should do, and as the minutes ticked away spasmodic fighting was still breaking out on various areas of the terracing. The players, meanwhile, had become superfluous and both teams were locked in their dressing-rooms. The Liverpool players were stunned and sickened by what they had seen and worried about the welfare of their wives and girlfriends in the stand above. At one stage I remember casting my eyes around the room and realising – as if for the first time – just how young some of our players were. A couple looked little more than kids, confused and on the verge of panic, and I can only imagine that the scene was similar to a war-time trench minutes after a group of teenage soldiers have returned from their first taste of battle. I'll never forget the face of Sammy Lee, the Liverpudlian. Tears were streaming down his face, mostly because of the shame that was being cast on the city of which he was so proud.

Reports were reaching us all the time and from a variety of different sources. Soon we were aware not only of the staggering size of the death toll but also of the fact that the victims were mainly Italians. Kenny Dalglish told the press afterwards that we had never been told about fatalities, but that was a lie. I still don't know why he chose to mislead people in this way because I for one have always been prepared to stand up and say that I knew people had died and despite that I still felt the match should be played.

The Italians captain, Gaetano Scirea, was asked by UEFA if he would be prepared to appeal over the public address system for calm on the terraces. A few minutes later the same request was put to me. At the time I understood that the Juventus players wanted the match to be called off and had made their feelings known to the officials. Nevertheless Scirea did go out and appeal to the Italian fans for calm and when it came to my turn I decided to take our bodyguard Tony Tye along with me for protection. The sprint to the PA position was one of the most frightening experiences of my life, with the Italian fans throwing missiles and hissing and spitting at me. The end of the stadium where the fighting had broken out was like an inner-city battleground with the concrete terracing broken up in many places. As I moved to take the microphone the UEFA official thrust a piece of paper into my hand and told me to read it out.

Luckily I scanned the text before I started because I couldn't believe what they wanted me to say. The giste was that the game would get underway in a few minutes' time if the fans settled down but that in the event of any more trouble the referee would abandon it. There was no way I was prepared to go along with this and told the official as much. I said I would willingly address the crowd but that I must be allowed to do so in my own words. The threat to abandon the game seemed as bad as the idea that it shouldn't start in the first place. In the end they let me do what I wanted and although I cannot remember exactly what I said, it was a general appeal for sanity and calm.

Back in the dressing-room it was clear that the other players had now been told the match was going ahead and I tried my best to calm them down, assuring them that the police had established control and that we would be far enough away from the terraces to be safe from attack. It would have been pointless in view of what had happened for the management to have tried to motivate us for the game so instead they told us to go out and get through it as best we could.

The match itself was a farce and I have no intention of spending any time describing it in detail. It is sufficient to say that it was played out in an unreal atmosphere and that from the start it was clear to me that there could be only one winner. When Ronnie Whelan was clearly fouled inside the box in the first half the Swiss referee, Daina, waved away our appeals for a penalty, and then in the second half when Gary Gillespie conceded a foul five yards outside the penalty area the referee pointed to the spot allowing Michel Platini to score the only goal of the game. Not a Liverpool voice was raised in protest at the decision, there would have been no point. Juventus had won that game before the first ball was kicked and – although I will never be able to prove it – I have subsequently learned from a number of reliable sources that a UEFA official had been overheard to say that on no account must Liverpool be allowed to win the game. When some of his decisions are analysed, the impartiality of the referee must be called into question.

However, for us the final whistle was the only sound we wanted to hear and as the Juventus players went through the motions of a victory celebration we trudged back to our dressing-room, anxious for news about our families, who had witnessed the whole horror of the evening from their seats in the main stand. Most of the women were in tears as we met up on the team coach. They had been sitting up in the stand since shortly after we arrived at the ground with only Liverpool's commercial manager, Kenny Addison, to offer male support. The entire night of shame had unfolded before their eyes and as a group of 16 well-dressed British women in the centre of the main stand they were soon identified as the wives and girlfriends of the players.

Their experience at the hands of the Italian supporters was far more traumatic than anything we had had to face. They were abused and spat upon and Paul Walsh's girlfriend Melissa was manhandled by a distraught Juventus fan as she made her way back from the toilet, and was forced to look down at the rows of corpses laid out behind the stand. I was horrified when I listened to what they had been made to sit through and was in awe of their restraint under such vile provocation. I was thankful only that there had been no children in the party. Indeed, my own ten-year-old son Ashley had been pestering me to allow him to come on the trip – imagine how relieved I felt that, although tempted to relent, I had in the end refused.

The club's sponsors had arranged a meal for us after the game and although no one was really in the mood, we went along because nobody could face going back to the hotel either. Even by the end of the evening the full implications of what had happened had still not really sunk in. The entire Liverpool party had descended into a state of deep shock. Defeat in the European Cup final was the last thing on anyone's mind as the awareness dawned that we were at the centre of a major disaster which would dominate world news and focus unprecedented attention on the game of football; the way it is organised and the social diseases that it has spawned. Many felt the game had needed a radical shake-up for some time, now one thing was all too clear – after the Brussel's massacre something had to be done – just what, though, we were yet to find out.

3
The Inquest

Nobody got much sleep that night, but there wasn't any talking done either. Everyone had their own thoughts to contend with, and the mental images from an evening that had started promising to be one of the most memorable of our careers and had ended in tatters – a nightmare that would haunt each and every one of us for the rest of our lives.

The next morning I awoke from a shallow doze feeling as though I'd lost a close relative. The phone in the room was ringing within minutes, reporters wanting my immediate reaction to newspaper stories I had yet to read. Sue bravely fielded all enquiries, telling people politely but firmly that I had no comment to make. Certainly I had nothing to say, words couldn't describe the way I was feeling ... after all I'd had a starring role in a real life horror movie.

Downstairs the foyer was packed with journalists and television crews. The sports reporters and feature-writers who had been with us the day before had now been joined by a breed entirely new to me, the newsmen looking for front page material. Fortunately the Liverpool party kept to its original schedule and made a swift getaway home. I can honestly say that I've never been so relieved to see the back of a city.

Back on Merseyside the club had scheduled a news conference. It had been arranged before the European Cup final and I can only think that the original idea had been to show off the triumphant winners or to temper the disappointment of defeat by unveiling a new manager. Understandably, though, the events of the previous evening had put paid to any such carefully laid plans and instead we found ourselves facing questions about the behaviour of our fans, our feelings about the decision to go ahead with the game despite the tragedy and our thoughts about the future. Overnight, Liverpool Football Club, for so long one of the few bright spots on an otherwise dismal Merseyside landscape, had become the scourge of the nation. The players quickly went their separate ways, their season over, with a few weeks' break in which to come to terms with what had happened. Now it was the turn of the club management to face up to consequences of football's night of shame.

The first repercussions came quickly. No sooner had UEFA announced that it would be holding a full enquiry into the tragedy then the English Football Association leapt in and announced that it was withdrawing all English clubs from European competition in the following season. Shocked and ashamed as I was about what had happened, I just couldn't believe that the FA would do such a thing. In one fell swoop they had destroyed the future ambitions of a whole string of clubs including Second Division Norwich City, who had qualified for Europe for the very first time. It seemed that the FA was acknowledging that the Liverpool fans had been solely to blame for the Brussel's riot but that the punishment should be borne by everyone.

I could accept neither point because as the dust settled on the incident and the comments and eye-witness reports became less charged with emotion and more considered it emerged that a minority of Liverpool supporters in an area adjacent to the Italian enclosure had been subjected to considerable provocation and had been bombarded with missiles in the two hours leading up to the game. It was their retaliatory charge and the mass retreat of the Italian fans that had brought too much pressure to bear on the dividing wall. The Belgian police, hopelessly ineffective in their management of the rival groups of fans up until this point, then failed to realise the scale of the catastrophe and sent their riot squads into the area instead of ambulance-men. Many of those who died suffocated and could probably have been pulled clear had the emergency services been alerted sooner.

Then there was the question of the suitability of the venue itself. UEFA had chosen the stadium but it was in a dreadfully run-down condition, the crumbling terraces providing concrete for the missiles, and there was no adequate means of segregating the fans – something that has been commonplace in stadiums the length and breadth of Europe for as long as I can remember. Sad though the fact may be, in this day and age you just cannot afford to allow 58,000 football fans to mingle freely.

So what about the role of the Belgian authorities? It turned out that the fans in the area where the fighting broke out had bought their tickets for the game in Brussels, so obviously no consideration had been given to the likely implications of allowing rival fans to share the same area of terracing. Finally we must consider the role of the police, whose numbers were always inadequate for the occasion and who, when things began to get out of hand at first, failed to call up reinforcements quickly enough, then hampered any rescue operation by drafting in a riot squad. Later still they allowed pockets of violence to continue and appeared either reluctant or unable to intervene.

But even after taking into account all these factors the Football Association still chose to make the big gesture, believing I suppose that by being seen to make the first move they might avoid possibly harsher judgement when the time came. How wrong can you be? Instead of waiting for the outcome of the enquiry, UEFA followed the FA's lead with some instant judgements of its own: an indefinite ban from European competition for all English clubs and an even stiffer three extra years for Liverpool once the blanket ban is lifted.

At a stroke, UEFA has wrecked the European dreams of at least half the Liverpool squad on the grounds of age, and has forced the young stars to reconsider their futures at the club and perhaps be tempted by the prospect of playing their football abroad. Furthermore, the European ban has jeopardised the whole financial structure of a club that has consistently gambled on European success as a way of off-setting any losses from the domestic season. Liverpool, for a number of reasons, have never been able to attract the same sort of average attendances as Manchester United and it has been the revenue from successive successful European Cup campaigns that has enabled the club to compete with its more glamorous rival on equal terms. By snatching away that potential source of income, UEFA has taken a step that could change the whole face of the club. The wages structure at Anfield is geared to European competition and in recent years some of the biggest stars in the game have been attracted to Liverpool rather than to the other top clubs because they felt they stood more chance of winning European medals. With a footballer's career as short as it is, any player can be forgiven for wanting the best possible opportunities – sadly at the moment Liverpool more than any other top club is unable to promise anything.

In the days following the disaster the newspapers were eager for any new angle on the story. The club chairman John Smith grabbed the headlines one morning when he stated that he had evidence to support a theory that the violence had been sparked off not by Liverpool supporters but by right-wing political extremists from the London area. He based his theory on the fact that tickets for the ill-fated section of terracing had not been on sale through the official supporters' club and the thugs would therefore have found it easy to obtain them and then get into the ground masquerading as genuine fans. His claims were apparently thoroughly investigated but the authorities could find no concrete evidence to support them.

A few mornings later I opened another paper to discover that Bruce Grobbelaar and myself were apparently so affected by the Brussels disaster that we were seriously thinking about quitting the game. I was amazed because, first of all, I had not answered the telephone to anyone since returning home and secondly, the idea of giving up had never occurred to me. I had retreated behind my front door to reflect on the tragedy and to consider the way forward in the light of Kenny Dalglish's appointment as team manager. Phil Neal had never been a quitter and wasn't about to become one now. Bruce, I later learned, was paid a few pounds for his contribution to the article so couldn't really complain if he was misquoted, but when he returned from his so-called 'think it all over' holiday in America there was certainly no talk about retiring.

The 1985-86 season began with English football on trial. The club ban on European competition had not been extended to the national side but with the European Championships scheduled for 1988 UEFA weren't slow to remind the English FA that any further incidents of crowd violence would almost certainly lead to expulsion from that tournament. The politicians had become involved in the debate and theories about the best solution abounded from all directions. The clubs dismissed the idea of identity cards as impractical and for their part urged the Government to spend some of the millions of pounds earned from the football pools on the improvement of facilities at stadiums. The Government counter-punched, saying that it was up to football in general and the clubs in particular to get their financial house in order like any other private industry, and the £900,000 transfer of Gary Lineker from Leicester City to Everton did nothing to convince the Government that the game was impoverished.

Many people have theories about how to tackle the problems of soccer hooliganism. Some demand stiffer and more consistent sentencing from the courts, while others advocate the introduction of better facilities and the development of a greater family atmosphere at grounds in an effort to isolate the villains. First and foremost, though, I believe the Football Association and the Football League must get together with the representatives of the clubs and reach a firm agreement on one particular strategem. All clubs would then agree to take part in the experiment for a certain period of time so that its success or otherwise could be properly assessed. Until someone is prepared to spearhead this sort of concerted initiative I'm convinced the problem of soccer hooliganism will remain with us.

The Brussels tragedy shocked the nation and there were many who believed it was the lesson the fans needed to learn, but again they were wrong. The soccer thug is either a mindless moron whose interest is in gang warfare rather than in football or a political agitator whose aim is to stretch the forces of law and order in any way he can. For a while the hooligans were a little subdued, but by the turn of the year – less than nine months after the Heysel Stadium disaster – they were creeping back.

To a degree incidents were hushed up by both the clubs and the authorities because UEFA had promised to review its ban and no one wanted them to hear anything that might alert them to the fact that we were still not on top of the problem. However, any hopes of keeping the lid on were dashed at Anfield, of all places, in February 1986 when Manchester United were the visitors. There a hooligan sprayed the United squad with an ammonia-like chemical as they stepped down from their coach. A number of players were affected but worse still, a young boy's eyes were smarting so badly that he had to taken to hospital. The incident happened when the BBC's cameras were at the ground for a live edition of *Match of the Day* and occurred right in front of a reporter: there was no way it could be hushed up and hooliganism was back on the front pages once again. Liverpool's chairman, anxious I suppose to deflect more unwanted attention away from his club's, fans went public with an allegation that manager Kenny Dalglish had been hit by a can as the club had left Old Trafford after a previous game, and slowly but surely over the next few days a more accurate picture of what had really been happening since Brussels began to emerge.

I'm no astrologer so as I write this I cannot possibly predict what UEFA will decide to do. I think they've found a convenient scapegoat in the form of the English clubs for a problem that is in no way confined to these shores. By moving so quickly after the incident they managed to pull a smokescreen over their own highly suspect role in the whole sad affair. It remains to be seen whether they will ever be brought to task for their inadequacies.

To have ended my European football career in such desperately tragic circumstances is something I shall never be able to forget. Inevitably, however hard I might try, it must cloud my memories of so many good times. At home I have a video library containing a permanent record of the high spots and indeed some of the low spots of my decade at Liverpool. The last one in the collection is marked 29 May 1985, Liverpool v Juventus, European Cup final, Heysel Stadium, Brussels. I've never watched it and, to my dying day, I never will.

4
In The Beginning

I've been football crazy for as long as I can remember. I was kicking a ball around almost soon as I could walk. In the afternoon and at weekends I used to spend every spare minute down on the local park and at night, along with the other lads in the neighbourhood, I'd be kicking around one of those plastic 'Frido' balls under the street lamps. Things were different in those days. For lads of my age and older football was an obsession, perhaps because there wasn't a lot else on offer ... especially where I lived. What is more, football was still the nation's number one talking point and a Saturday wasn't complete without either playing or watching a game.

There was a football tradition in our family. My Dad had been a useful player before the War and had got as far as trials with West Bromwich Albion. Sadly, though, his health was on the decline when I was growing up so he was unable to play an active part in helping my progress as a schoolboy player. I was brought up in Irchester, a small rural community just outside Northampton and there were plenty of Neals about. I had so many cousins that I never got around to learning all of their names but the great advantage was that they did offer me an instant introduction to those all-important scratch games on the local park. Sunday afternoon was the time for the big kickabout and if offered the chance to put into practice skills observed from the terraces the previous afternoon. I started going along and getting a game – thanks to the cousins – when I was about seven.

They were rough and tumble affairs with coats down at each end for goals. The age gap meant that I was happy to turn out for whichever was a player short and I remember hanging around each week as the older lads turned up and keeping my fingers crossed that there would be an odd number by kick-off time. More often than not there was a vacancy for me and that meant mixing it with the 15-and 16-year-olds. For a while they gave me the runaround but at the same time I was learning some important lessons about how to look after myself. I was quite well-built for my age and a strong kicker of the ball whenever it came my way. More importantly, those Sunday afternoons gave me a head start when it came to games at school.

Most of the lads in Irchester dreamt of becoming footballers in much the same way as most kids do but we had a ready-made hero right on our doorstep. Bobby Tebbutt must have been about 20 and he was on the books of Northampton Town. In our eyes that gave him superstar status. Most evenings we'd hang around at the end of the street waiting for him to get off the bus on his way back from training. Naturally we'd always have a ball with us and he'd often stop for a quick kickabout before going in for his tea. The way in which he hung on to the ball and the ease with which he made sure none of us got a sniff of it put him in a different class. Often I would wonder whether I'd ever get to play as well as Bobby Tebbutt. The records show he made around 50 appearances for 'The Cobblers' before injury cut short his career.

At infant school there was no organised football but the games in the playground were treated every bit as seriously as the big match on Sunday afternoons. Mostly I organised the sides and some days it was all we could do to wait for the bell at the end of school. The playground was ideally suited to the game, tapering towards a couple of posts that formed a natural goalmouth at one end. Usually, the two teams had been sorted out beforehand during whispered exchanges behind the teacher's back. All that remained was to persuade the girls to go to the other end of the yard and the match could get underway. My height and strength ensured that I regularly got my share of the goals.

My footballing career really started once I'd made the move up to the juniors. There was a school team but when I started asking about it the other lads just laughed. It was dominated by ten-and eleven-year-olds, the boys on the verge of secondary school. At eight, they said, I'd got no chance. Well, they were proved wrong because just after the start of my first year there the school team found itself with some sort of selection crisis. I and another boy from the year above had been making a mark in our class matches and were summoned to see the PE teacher. Great, I thought, I must be odds on for a trial, but I soon discovered he had nothing so grand in mind. The pair of us were told to don our boots and follow him out on to the school field. There, on a damp Friday afternoon in October, my competitive career was launched. This soccer mastermind ordered each of us to take three penalties at the school goalie. I scored the lot, was handed a shirt and told I'd be in the side for the next day's game ... the youngest pupil ever to appear for the school team.

Little did I know then that in years to come I'd step up to take two penalties that would enable me to win two European Cup Winners' medals. Nevertheless, that day the prize – a place in the school team – was equally important to me. I remember walking home that evening not knowing in which position I would be playing and wondering where the penalty-taking contest fitted in. It crossed my mind that the standard must be pretty tough if penalty kicks were of such prime importance! I must have checked my boots a dozen times that night and by the time I had finished they were polished to perfection. I got my Mum to run an iron over my kit and I hardly slept a wink.

Ironically my debut for the school team was similar to so many of the important milestones in my footballing career

– totally unexpected. Many managers firmly believe this is the best way to 'blood' inexperienced players because the shock of the last-minute news prevents them from freezing on the big occasion. However, with the best will in the world I cannot count the teacher in charge of my first school team as one of the great soccer brains of his generation. I can't remember the school we faced in that first match or the final score, only that I played at inside right and scored a goal. Looking back through the mists of time I would have to fall back on that classic quote that has been a lifeline to generations of footballers: 'It just came across, I hit it, and the next thing I knew it was in the back of the net, Brian'!

Getting into the school team was the one chance I needed. I kept my place in the side and never missed a game throughout my junior years. You see, that record of consistency I was so proud of at Liverpool goes back a long way! Once I moved to the football-mad Wollaston Secondary School, the game began to take over my life. By some fantastic coincidence the right calibre of players came together at the right time and we swept everything before us. There wasn't a major school trophy that we didn't win and at one time no less than six members of this same school team were representing the County. I couldn't get enough football and quickly signed up with one of the top youth sides in the area, Wellingborough Celtic. The routine was punishing – a game for the school on Saturday mornings, the club in the afternoon and, of course, the ritual kickaround on Sundays – but who was complaining? Certainly not me!

The youth team at Wellingborough was an extension of a proper club set-up and we trained twice a week in a local gym. The emphasis was on fitness and ball skills and, to their credit, the people who ran the side never tried to complicate the issue with tactics. Their philosophy was that football was first and foremost a game to be enjoyed and if you could win at the same time so much the better.

We were encouraged to go out and compete for every ball and they developed in us a total belief in team spirit. The side's record is a testimony to their endeavours. In the years the team was together, we won everything going with the possible exception of the Boat Race. My Mum couldn't find enough room in the china cabinet for all the trophies I was bringing home.

By the time I was 14, the professional clubs had begun to show an interest in the club and the scouts started to appear on the touchline at our games. I was still playing mainly as an inside forward and scoring my fair share of goals, but the real star of the side was my striking partner Paul Shoemark. He possessed that little bit of extra flair – nowadays I'd describe it as greed – and he never failed to catch the eye of the professional observer. At 15, Paul was a year older than me and had star quality written all over him. His father was pushing him all the way and when he made the England schoolboys side everyone thought he might go on to become the next Bobby Charlton. He scored a goal at Wembley in one of the first televised schoolboy internationals and almost every first division club wanted to sign him. In the end he chose Tottenham Hotspur.

I've never been able to find out who tipped them off, but it seems someone told the Tottenham staff that there was another promising youngster up Wellingborough way because a few months later I received a letter inviting me to a trial at the club's Cheshunt training ground. What a day it turned out to be! I played well in the game and was given the red-carpet treatment with a guided tour of White Hart Lane. I didn't realise it at the time, but I was being subjected to much the same subtle pressure as most of the top schoolboys. I met coaches who talked glibly about plans for the youth team to go on a European tour in the close season and naturally I was completely taken in – a European tour! At that time I hadn't even got a passport.

The clincher was a meeting at the end of the day with the great Bill Nicholson. For me it was like being summoned to an audience with God. Just a few years earlier Spurs had pulled off their great double triumph and they remained one of the nation's top clubs. They could take their pick of the country's best schoolboy players yet here was the man himself offering me terms as an apprentice. It was like a dream come true. I mumbled something about having to talk things over with my parents and Mr Nicholson said there was no hurry. I rushed home to break the news, expecting their agreement to be a mere formality – so much for the naïveté of youth. My parents were both level-headed people. They knew I wanted a career in the game but they were also aware of the enormous gulf between signing as an apprentice and actually making it as a full professional. They insisted that I talk over the future with my PE teacher, Rod Derry, who'd been an inspiration to me at Wollaston.

His advice was sensible and to the point but certainly not what I wanted to hear. I wasn't really interested in common sense, just in my desire to play football for Spurs. He warned me about the enormous gamble I would be taking and the statistics he used to back up his argument were frightening. The percentage of players who actually make it through to the first team at any club is very small compared with the number of lads taken on in the first place. Rod argued that I should stay at school and complete my education. He felt that if Spurs were interested in me now, then as long as my form didn't suffer, they would still want to sign me a year later. It was the toughest decision of my life, and it was made worse by the fact that Paul had had no such misgivings and signed straight away. Reluctantly, yet appreciating the wisdom of Rod's advice, I turned Tottenham down and stuck with my studies. The end result was five GCE 'O' levels which, at one point seven years later, I was to consider more valuable than any medal or cup in my trophy cabinet.

Nottingham Forest invited me for trials during my final year at school but didn't offer me an apprenticship when the time came so instead I ended up signing for my local club, Northampton Town. I'd been training with the youngsters at the County Ground for a couple of seasons but I never really thought I'd end up joining them full-time. After all, I had been an England schoolboy triallist and just a year earlier had attracted the attention of one of the most famous clubs in the country. In the end, though, I was grateful for the opportunity and the chance to follow in the footsteps of Bobby Tebbutt.

Nottingham Forest I could take or leave, but what hurt me most at the time was the fact that, in true football tradition, Tottenham didn't come back and neither did any of the other big clubs for that matter. There was a strong rumour at one stage that Arsenal were about to make a move for me but it remained just that – a rumour.

I often wondered how my old mate Paul was getting on in the rarified atmosphere of White Hart Lane. I heard little from him at the time but later I realised that his problems were far greater than mine. Even amongst the top-class young players at White Hart Lane, he was regarded by the coaching staff as something extra special. They would talk openly about having discovered a real jewel, a young player who would make it to the very top, and the result was resentment from the other apprentices who tended to make his life a misery. As a consequence, his confidence suffered and although he did go on to sign as a pro, a year later he had still not made the breakthrough and time was running out. He managed a few reserve games for Spurs but finally they released him. Officially, he didn't make the grade, but in reality, like Wayne Harrison a generation later, he was a victim of the system. Sadly, Paul then failed to come to terms with top-flight non-league football and eventually drifted out of the game completely. He confirmed my teacher's grim prediction. On the face of it he joined a top club and sacrificed everything for the chance. In reality he was pitting himself against the very cream of the nation's schoolboy talent, and although I don't blame him for that, looking back I realise I made the right decision.

The top clubs have their pick of the youngsters. They coax them with great promises but in the end they have to deliver on the club's terms. Too often youngsters are taken on at 16 only to be rejected at 19 or 20, their lives in turmoil. Many fail to recover from the shock and never realise their true potential. Often these same players need only special encouragement or are late developers who could be expected to break into the first team in their early 20s. Nowadays, with the advent of Government sponsored YTS scheme, the situation has become even worse because the clubs are not even spending their own money any more. The smaller clubs take on more teenagers that they know what to do with and the art of spotting a youngster with true potential has largely become a thing of the past, because for the first time clubs can afford to take on kids with question-marks hanging over their heads on the off-chance that they might make the grade. But I'm afraid that all this leads to is even more disappointment for the hopeful young player when the time comes for the club to make its decision.

Liverpool is no exception. I'm not suggesting for a minute that the club abuses the YTS system, merely that it doesn't take its obligations to young players seriously enough. In recent years from among the apprentices only Phil Thompson and Sammy Lee have emerged to establish themselves as first team players. So many others have been thrown on to the scrapheap like my mate Paul without a qualification to their name and the confidence knocked right out of them. If my son Ashley ever shows enough promise, I'm determined to encourage him not only to complete his studies but also to start with a smaller club. That way he can develop at his own pace, enjoy a greater rapport with the first team players and generally learn the harsh realities of football without becoming permanently damaged ... looking back I'm sure Paul Shoemark would be the first to agree with me.

5

Northampton – Life as a 'Cobbler'

It needed a bump start, but the souped-up motor scooter that had served me so well since I wisely invested ten pounds for its purchase finally spluttered into life for the short ride into Northampton. It was August 1967 and I was finally about to achieve my schoolboy ambition and swap the textbooks for life as a professional footballer. I had no illusions about the scale of the challenge and was determined to succeed. My father had died a few months earlier and I knew that from now on it would all be down to me. He'd been ill for some time and I think I inwardly feared the worst, but it had been good to have his support and now that it wasn't there any more it just strengthened my resolve to succeed. Others had done it so why shouldn't I?

I was in good time for the mid-afternoon appointment with manager Ron Flowers and Dave Bowen, the club secretary, but I needed to be because neither the old scooter nor its rider were best known for their turn of speed. Then, just around the corner from the ground, disaster struck. The only thing I remember is a crowd of anxious faces gathered above me as I lay spreadeagled in the road. The mangled wreck of my precious scooter was lying in a pool of petrol several yards away and slewed broadside was a car with a hefty dent in its front wing. I had several cuts and bruises and it was obvious that, despite my dazed protests, an ambulance was on its way and I was heading for the hospital rather than Ron Flowers' office. The signing would have to wait! A thorough check-up showed nothing too serious – apparently my head took most of the impact – but all the same it was a battered Phil Neal who finally hobbled into the County Ground a few days later to complete the formalities and become the club's newest apprentice. I was no stranger to the set-up by that time but the manager's face was full of concern ... concern that he may have signed a teenage cripple instead of a promising young footballer.

Ron Flowers, blond and fresh-faced, looked no different from the days when he was a mighty swashbuckling wing half with Wolverhampton Wanderers. Just a year earlier he had been a member of England's winning World Cup squad and now he was trying his hand at management. Ron spelled out the terms: ten pounds a week during the playing season and eight pounds a week during the summer. Then he dealt with my duties: sweeping the terraces after match day; mopping out the dressing-rooms; sorting out the kit for the senior players and cleaning their boots. Oh! And training and playing in matches as well of course ... if I could find the time.

There were about half a dozen of us on the ground staff in those days and the term was a particularly apt description of our role in the life of the club. We were expected at the ground an hour before the full professionals to make sure everything was laid out ready for them and then once they were satisfied we went off to training. We used the same field as the others, but trained separately. Then, once training was over at lunch-time, we went under the supervision of the groundsman for the rest of the afternoon. It was a tough life for a kid, with few perks, and it's funny how some of the smallest matters took on a special significance in that sort of environment. I'll never forget the time Ron Flowers threw me a pair of his old boots and asked if I could find any use for them. There were holes in both toes and as far as he was concerned they were beyond repair. Even in that sorry state, though, they were a class above anything I could afford and so I nipped to the cobbler's around the corner from the ground and persuaded him to patch them up. Those boots became special to me, a good luck symbol if you like, and I managed to coax another two season's service out of them. Ironically, years later at Liverpool where the major manufacturers were constantly offering us substantial cash backhanders to wear their products, the boots were never a patch (excuse the pun) on those hand-me-downs from Ron Flowers.

There was one area in which the youngsters had the upper hand on the pros, however, and that was when it came to handing out the training kit. Personal hygiene didn't figure on the list of priorities at the County Ground in those days and the club specified that training kit should be laundered only once a week. In the winter months with the mud ankle-deep on the training field the players would return to the dressing-room and throw their filthy gear in a massive, steaming heap in the middle of the floor. The thankless task for the apprentices was to sort the strips out and to put them in the boiler-room to dry. Next day, with the shirts and socks dry but as stiff as boards, the young lads would have to beat them against a wall before hanging them on pegs ready for the pros. Sometimes when the weather was particularly bad the club would relent and lay out two or three clean strips. These would be snapped up by the apprentices first thing in the morning leaving the familiar filthy stuff for the others. Naturally the protests would be long and abusive, and the tackles during the practice match particularly late, but it was worth it. Having first choice of the training kit remained the second most important perk for the Northampton apprentice.

The best perk of all, though, was as rare as Christmas but equally welcome. As I've already mentioned, our wages were paltry and any bonus was gratefully received. The best windfalls came on a Monday afternoon as we swept the cigarette packets and sweet wrappers off the terraces.

Occasionally we'd find coins, coppers mostly but sometimes the odd half-crown, and we split everything six ways so that nobody lost out. Then one particular Monday as I was sweeping behind the goal I came across the biggest find to date – a ten shilling *note*! Down to the local chippy we went and an unsuspecting spectator provided six hungry apprentices with the best meal they'd had in weeks.

Three years before I joined Northampton, the club had been at the very top, rising from the fourth to the first division in successive seasons. Now they were on the return journey. Ron Flowers had inherited a fading side and was forced, I suppose more by circumstances than choice, to adopt a youth policy. I was the first beneficiary, becoming the youngest player to appear for the club when I made my debut in the autumn of my first season as an apprentice. I was still an inside forward in those days and for a while first-team opportunities were limited. What is more, any thoughts I might have had about life becoming any easier thanks to the early breakthrough were quickly dispelled by the senior pros who, if anything, seemed hell-bent on making things even tougher. Their idea of keeping a young lad's feet on the ground was to kick him even harder during training and the net result was that I seemed to sustain more knocks from my own team-mates from Monday to Friday than from any of those opponents on a Saturday who considered it their mission in life to prove to a fresh-faced 16-year-old that he had stumbled into a man's game.

I was barely established in the first team when Ron Flowers got the sack. He was judged to have failed in his struggle to stop the rot and the directors made him pay the inevitable price. I was shattered. Ron was the man who had signed me; given me a pair of cast-off boots and then my break in the first team. I owed him a lot and his dismissal was a tremendous blow. Dave Bowen, a permanent fixture at the club in one form or another, took over for a while – more of him later – and then the directors

Rome 1984 – a goal, a penalty and the European Cup. Even Bruce was a hero!
Daily Mirror

TOP: *Brussels 1985 – Juventus fans hurl missiles at anyone within range.* Colorsport

BOTTOM: *With the dead and injured all around them, the fighting fans spill over on to the track around the pitch.* Colorsport

TOP: *Team orders were out of the question – we just had to get through the game as best we could.* Colorsport

BOTTOM: *The exchange of pennants – earlier we'd both appealed to the fans for calm.* Colorsport

TOP: *Ron Greenwood's World Cup Squad – had it not been for the players' persuasion he would never have made it to Spain.* Bob Thomas

BOTTOM: *Spain 1982 – Don Howe explains the plan as the Spanish police watch over us.* Bob Thomas

Another time, another place as John Gregory and I concentrate on one of Bobby 'Mogadon' Robson's team talks. Bob Thomas

ABOVE: *Getting in that vital tackle – this time to rob Eric Gates of Ipswich.*

RIGHT: *It's tough at the top but you can't afford to give Frank Stapleton anything – even your head! (FA Cup semi-final, Liverpool v Arsenal 1980.)*
Bob Thomas

ABOVE: *John Robertson crossing the ball and reminding me that I'm a yard too slow even for him.*
Colorsport

LEFT: *Tommy Hutchinson – football's 'spiderman' – jinks his way into my very own web.*
Mulvaney Brooks

TOP: *Steve Heighway pays a personal tribute to my football brain.*
Harry Ormesher

BOTTOM: *Natasha with a superstar. Kevin Keegan is looking on.*

turned to Bill Baxter, the former Ipswich Town defender. Baxter arrived at the County Ground with the reputation of a hard man; a moody but hot-headed Scot who acted first and thought it over later. He had played over 400 games for Ipswich Town before a dressing-room brawl with manager Bobby Robson ended with Baxter being transferred to Hull City for £12,500.

Baxter joined Northampton with the club stranded in the Third Division relegation zone. Panic was in the air, particularly the air breathed by the directors. To everyone's amazement the board offered a staggering five-year contract as trainer to a local physiotherapist, Charlie McCormack. I say staggering because Charlie was a former army Sergeant Major and fitness fanatic with no experience whatsoever of professional football. Baxter, by reputation, had not been the world's keenest trainer when he was a player and as a manager his enthusiasm for the daily session was non-existent. The grind was left to Charlie and, even to my inexperienced eyes, the sessions were a joke. His knowledge of the game came from two distinct sources: the coaching manuals of the 1950s and the pages of *Charles Buchan's Football Monthly*. He belonged to the school that believed football was about anything but the ball itself.

Charlie was into fitness and with fitness came running and PT and with running and PT came the charts – 'Charlie's Charts' as they soon became known were the means by which the performance of each and every member of the first team squad was monitored. It was a crazy situation because Charlie, who looked for all the world like something left over from the Army Game, was a first rate physic and would have been happy enough to fulfil that role, yet instead the board in its ignorance and Baxter through his laziness had elevated him to the point where he took day-to-day responsibility for the training routines and coaching sessions. Under Charlie we could go from Monday to Friday without so much as a glimpse of a football. 'It makes you hungry for it come Saturday afternoon', he would snap at anyone brave enough to question his methods. On the contrary, by Saturday we'd forgotten what to do with it but what could I say when more experienced players were prepared to accept the regime?

Instead we would run, run until we thought our legs were about to drop off. We'd jog around the field to improve our stamina, sprint to show that we'd got pace and skip to prove that we were nimble. Charlie even got a couple of the apprentices to knock up a dozen sets of wooden steps, each exactly a foot high because he'd read somewhere that this was the optimum height for improving the strength of one particular leg muscle. Baxter, meanwhile, would mooch around the ground glaring and growling at anyone unfortunate enough to stray into his line of vision.

On match days, Charlie would commandeer the apprentices who weren't playing and give them notebooks, pencils and seats in the main stand. His brief was simple, the lads were expected to record each movement of every Northampton player out on the field. He'd worked out a code, a continuous line represented a run, a dotted line a sprint and a broken line with dots and dashes was a weaving dribble. Over the weekend he would process the information and by Monday he would be able to give the manager his considered opinion on who had been shirking and who had played his heart out. We managed to fix him once, though, when we got hold of one of the notebooks and placed six crosses in a line with five more in a line below. Charlie could make neither head nor tail of it until someone pointed out that the players had posed for a team photograph before the kick-off. Needless to say Charlie didn't see the joke.

All but one of us thought the system was a complete farce. The exception was a lad called Jimmy Johnson. He was like a chicken with no head, the sort of player who could run all day but had no brains. He was Charlie's kind of player but for the rest of us he was a complete waste of time. Jimmy couldn't play football at that level to save his life and everyone knew it but him. Week after week he'd have stinkers, but each afternoon as we trooped back into the dressing-room he'd make a big show of wringing out his shirt and complaining that he'd covered every blade of grass on the park but the other lads had let him down. Everyone knew what was happening, and most of the players took the mickey out of him, but come Monday and the team meeting who was Charlie's man of the match week after week? Yes, none other than Jimmy the brainless whirlwind – no wonder the slide continued and we plunged into the fourth division the very first season I was signed as a full-time pro.

Northampton was my local club and I'd always been a fan, but the County Ground during Bill Baxter's reign was a particularly depressing place to be. Few of the lads got along with him and most resented the way he threw his weight about – and by that time, with training but a distant memory, he had plenty of weight available. I remember being amazed by the lack of interest he showed in the job and his lethargic attitude was reflected in the players' attitude on the field. The team was playing badly with no real sense of direction and, understandably, the supporters were soon on our backs. I tried to steer clear of the dressing-room squabbles and keep out of the manager's way, but I'll never forget the one occasion I did fall foul of him because it was with far-reaching consequences.

Northampton had no money to speak of and overnight stays on the way to away games were out of the question. The one exception was Workington, where the distance involved made the journey a nightmare without a stop-over. The team hotel was in Kendal and we arrived there early on the Friday evening. We had a meal and then a few of the lads – myself included – decided to take a walk around the town. There were six of us on the jaunt and after about half an hour we came across a lively-looking pub in the town centre. We decided to pop in for a coke and got involved in a game of darts with a bunch of the local lads. Gradually the players drifted off and in the end there were only three of us left. Nevertheless we were on our way back to the hotel well before the boss's curfew. On the way out of the pub we must have been spotted by Baxter and Charlie who were probably out for a drink themselves.

Nothing was said until after the team's defeat the next day and then on the coach back to Northampton the manager started to get stuck in. He and Charlie must have ducked into that same pub because he had chapter and verse about our night out, the only difference was that the Coco-Colas we'd been drinking had suddenly become pints of bitter!

Baxter was throwing the book at me and I was speechless: a waster; unprofessional; letting my team-mates down; the lot – come to think of it, he must have been reciting the script from memory. He was in no mood to listen to my explanations even if I was telling the truth and in the end, insults exhausted, he pointed a finger at me and said: 'So that's it, Nealy, you're suspended for a week without pay!'.

I was gutted. I had just turned 20, was newly-married and absolutely desperate for cash. Sue and I were struggling to keep up with the mortgage repayments on our first home and the idea of losing a week's wages for something as innocent as that evening in the pub was devastating. Had the same thing happened years later I would have had the confidence to stand my ground and answer him back but I was still wet behind the ears and all I could think about was how the family would manage the following week. That night I crept into the house not knowing quite how to break the news to Sue. She hadn't been in Kendal to see for herself how innocent the evening had been so how was I to know that she'd believe my version of events?

As it turned out, though, her only concern – like mine –

was how we would get by. We talked things over and on Monday morning I was off to the employment exchange instead of the County Ground. Work must have been easier to come by in those days because in next to no time I had been fixed up with a job at a local agricultural firm churning out cattle cake. The job meant a five o'clock start in the morning and a long bus journey from Northampton out to the farm. Conditions there were foul and the smell was far worse than that in the 'Cobbler's' dressing-room on a wet winter's morning after a few of the lads had been out the night before. Beggars can't be choosers, though, and out of necessity I stuck it out, cursing Bill Baxter every minute of the working day. The irony was that when pay-day came around I actually ended up with more money in my wage packet for making cattle cake than I had ever earned from playing football.

The following Monday I reported back to the ground and everyone behaved as if nothing had happened. I didn't forget, though, and my respect for the manager had hit rock-bottom. I was leading the celebrations a few months later when his lack of commitment and poor attitude finally stretched the patience of the directors and they sacked him.

Looking back, the Kendal incident and Baxter's reaction to it summed up the man perfectly. He acted on impulse, without ever considering the validity of what he was doing or the consequences of his actions. On reflection, I'm sure my suspension would have been laughed out of court if I'd taken issue with him, and if he'd tried anything like that today, with the players' union as strong as it is, he would never have been allowed to get away with it. What is more, his action was totally unnecessary because instead of effectively sacking me for a week he could have fined me my wages and still made me train. As it happened, his pig-headed attitude enabled me to pick up a nice little bonus for the family purse.

Earning a living was one of the things that preoccupied

me most in those days. I would often lie awake at night worrying about how we were going to make ends meet. Even when I signed as a full-time pro and my wages went up to £20 a week, the cost of our modest lifestyle still outstripped the money coming in. Every little bonus helped and in the summer months of the close season I would take another job, which was often the means by which I avoided the cheques bouncing in the winter. Perhaps the only advantage of playing for an unsuccessful club was the fact that the season always ended with the last league game ... for us, Europe and close-season tours were merely things to dream about.

For a couple of summers I swapped jobs with Peter Willey, the Northampton cricketer. He'd found a position at a local shoe factory the previous winter and when his season started mine had finished so I took over the job. The arrangement suited the pair of us very well and luckily the management were happy too. Another year I got a job driving a van for a company which sold decorating materials. I was up at dawn to collect my orders and then spent the rest of the day driving the length and breadth of the county with my deliveries. One particular day I was way behind schedule and driving like a madman in an effort to catch up. I screeched to a halt outside the shop perched at the top of a steep hill. I rushed around the back and threw open the doors only to be greeted by a cascade of paint cans as they rolled out. There was a river of paint running down the gutter and I was halfway towards a box of tissues before I realised there was no point. I leapt back into the van sharpish and sped off into the distance instead. For years I could still see traces of paint on that particular street.

The disadvantage of a long break in the summer was the torturous grind of pre-season training, but fortunately the demise of Bill Baxter brought about a change of policy at the County Ground. His successor, Bill Dodgin Jnr, was a tracksuit manager in the best tradition and he wasted no time at all in shunting Charlie McCormick back to the treatment room. Suddenly there were balls on the training field again and the emphasis switched back from fitness at all costs to the basic skills. Bill was determined to get the club back on its feet but he was equally sure that the only way forward was through playing quality football. His was a refreshing approach to the game and his style suited me down to the ground, but unfortunately I'm not sure he was as convinced about me. I still considered myself an inside forward in those days and that's the position I started in at the beginning of his first full season in charge. I scored seven goals in the first eight games and for the first time in my career I was beginning to feel happy with the way I was playing. Two months in, however, one of the half-backs got injured and the manager drafted me into his position. By the time he was fit again the lad who had taken my place up front was playing too well to be dropped so Bill left out the full-back instead and played me at the back. I remained in the defence throughout the rest of the season and although I managed to score only one goal I still ended up the club's top scorer!

I'm convinced that my versatility and willingness to fill in were crucial factors in slowing down my progress in those early years. I was never given the chance to establish myself in any one position and I don't think an older player would have tolerated all the chopping and changing. As a youngster still finding my way in the game, I think I was too easy going, concerned more with getting regular first-team football than with worrying about playing in the right position.

It was this unsettled playing pattern coupled with the strain associated with life at an unsuccessful club that gradually started to eat away at my confidence. I began worrying about my form and the harder I tried to improve my game the more difficult things became. I knew I wasn't playing well but, try as I might, I couldn't seem to drag myself out of the rut. Eventually those first nagging feelings of self-doubt began and in next to no time I was questioning the whole idea of a career as a professional footballer.

6

'How Do You Fancy Liverpool?'

Monday 9 October 1974 turned out to be the most important day of my life yet I'd have laughed in the face of anyone who'd suggested as much as I scrambled around organising breakfast in the cluttered kitchen of our tiny terraced house on the outskirts of Northampton. It was a dismal autumn morning and things were even more chaotic than usual because Sue had been confined to hospital during the final weeks of pregnancy. Family and friends were helping in any way they could, but to be honest there were a few thistles popping up in life's bed of roses.

Looking back, it was an odd moment to be taking stock, but nevertheless that morning I was preoccupied with the career of P. Neal, professional footballer. Seven years with Northampton had given me a thorough grounding in the game but the facts were staring me in the face. I had one of the emptiest trophy cupboards in the game. The club had been relegated the very season I turned pro and since then had been struggling in Division Four. I'd become what is affectionately known in the game as a 'utility player'. In reality I think that's a loose tag to describe a player the manager's not quite sure what to do with. Until the previous Saturday I'd played only in all ten outfield positions, but when goalkeeper Alan Starling was carried off I seized the opportunity to complete the full set with an appearance as emergency 'keeper. With a name like Starling, I'd half expected him to reappear on the wing but no, he stayed in the dressing-room, and I pulled off a string of spectacular saves to ensure we won the game 3-1.

Up to my elbows in soapsuds and dirty dishes and with half an eye on the kitchen clock, I suppose I could have picked a better time to consider my future. However, consider it I did, and the prospects looked bleak. Although happily married with a daughter and another baby on the way, I was up to my neck in a mortgage on the £3,500 terraced house we called home. I was earning the princely sum of £50 a week – there weren't many win bonuses at Northampton – and that didn't leave much over for luxuries like food!

At 23 I was beginning to accept that the big time had passed me by, so what were the options? Week after week I'd join the rest of the lads in the dressing-room jokes about which big club had a scout at the County Ground and who was top of his wanted list. Privately I always hoped it might be me, but the football gossip column in the *Sunday People* – a tabloid transfer market in its own right – had never once mentioned me in dispatches. They were always reporting that Arsenal fancied this player or Newcastle were interested in someone else but of me, not a word. That column – compulsive reading for so many – was fast becoming repulsive reading for me.

You know, it's amazing the way some Fourth Division players behave. For many, tapping the commissionaire to let them flick through the envelopes to check which big clubs had asked for complimentary tickets was a vital part of their pre-match ritual. There was one particular player at Northampton who made a point of warming up in front of the main stand during the pre-match kickabout. He'd go on some of his best runs of the afternoon during those five minutes as he scanned the director's box for a familiar face.

A few weeks previously I'd attracted the attention of Aldershot. The *Sunday People* missed that startling piece of information but I doubt the Sports Editor bothered to carpet anybody because even I found the bid difficult to get excited about. What was the point? A new area, another house to buy, the same standard of football and same standard of living – low! The carrot they'd dangled to tempt me away from Northampton was an extra five pounds a week. Bury were courting me too, and that was a bit more interesting. They were in the heartland of English football and had produced some good players in their time, Colin Bell being a particular favourite. Their manager, Bobby Smith – obviously a shrewd judge of talent – had wanted to make a firm offer of £7,000 but apparently his chairman wasn't sure I was worth the money.

But there was also a third offer on the table, and as I coaxed my battered old Volkswagen into life I was beginning to think that it might be the most attractive. Kettering Town were then an ambitious Southern League outfit managed by 'Big' Ron Atkinson, and although he hadn't exactly made me an offer I couldn't refuse, I felt his approach warranted my full consideration. Ron wanted me as a part-time pro and said he could match what I was getting at Northampton. In the dim and distant past I'd pocketed five 'O' levels – although just which pocket I'd put them in I wasn't exactly sure – and there was a place waiting for me at Teacher Training College. Sue and I had discussed the offer at length. Even in those days Ron had a persuasive tongue. Although at Kettering his jewellery was more copper than gold, his shoes more Timpson than Gucci and his hair more ... well lets just say more, he was already something special. Along with Sue, I figured he was one of the few people who genuinely believed I could play. Perhaps going part-time was the answer to my problems.

The trusty Beetle showed 27 miles on the clock as I pulled into the car park at the County Ground. Actually it had done more than 100,000 but to celebrate the end of British Summer Time I'd put the clock back! It occurred to me that signing for Kettering might be the only way of putting together enough cash to buy a newer model. The irony was that Kettering had far more money to spread around than Northampton and Ron had made it pretty plain in our chats over the phone that there'd be enough in the till for a 'little signing-on fee' if I did decide to join him.

Locking the car – although God knows why I bothered – I was thinking about the difference a 'little signing-on fee' would make to my family life. To be honest, Ron's back-hander would have bought my house and given me more to show from football at the sweep of a pen than any number of years in the Fourth Division. I'd asked Ron for time to think about it but couldn't expect him to hang on for ever. In my head I really fancied the move, but in my heart I was finding it difficult to come to terms with the fact that I hadn't made it in the Football League. The advantages of joining Kettering were plain to see but it was still a tough decision to make.

Christmas seemed a good enough crossroads and I'd just about decided to give it until then when one of the lads spotted me and broke my train of thought: 'Phil, the boss is looking for you'. Summoned to Bill Dodgin's office first thing on a Monday morning? It must be a bollocking, I thought, as I made my way to the other end of the ground. I was going over Saturday's match in my mind. I'd spent most of the afternoon in goal so unless he was going to have a go at my handling there wasn't much else he could complain about. Alan Starling's goal kicks weren't in the same class as mine. On the other hand perhaps he wanted to keep me in goal until Starling was ready to fly again ... you know the old football saying, never change a winning team.

A quick tap on the door and then straight in. A neat bodyswerve took me past the heater behind the door – less nimble players would have fallen over it – and I was face to face with the boss. Bill looked up from his desk.

'How do you fancy Liverpool?' he asked.

Quick as a flash I was back at him:

'Who're they playing?'

He wasn't going to get me as easily as that, even on a Monday morning.

'You'd better sit down son', he added, ignoring my last sentence. He started to smile. Now that was unusual in itself because Bill wasn't a cheerful sort of bloke at the best of times and this was a Monday morning. 'They've made an offer, we've accepted and now its up to you', he said.

Apparently, Liverpool had watched me a couple of times during the past few weeks but hadn't made a final decision. Their scout, Geoff Twentyman, had been at the previous weekend's game and had recommended they should come in with a bid. I've always wondered how they could be sure of my ability on the strength of a game in which I spent the majority of my time in goal, but then again, football seems to work like that. Any normal Saturday I'd probably have had a stinker and nothing more would have been heard of Phil Neal.

Liverpool! In an instant, Kettering, Aldershot, Bury and Teacher Training College became things of the past. Now Anfield and football meant everything to me. 'When do we go?' I asked, unable to contain my excitement. It turned out they were expecting us that afternoon and Dave Bowen, the club secretary, was to drive me to Merseyside. Dave had been there when Bill broke the news and it was all he could do to persuade me to go home and change. He felt my 'golf' jeans – with their 18 holes – and the jumper which, if it had ever had a best, was well past it, might not be quite the right gear for the customary signing-on picture.

Back home I went and out came the wedding suit. I don't think I'd worn it since the big day and the flower in the lapel had wilted a bit, but what better occasion to bring it out of mothballs? I rushed around making arrangements with the family although the one person I couldn't get hold of was Sue. I was disappointed she couldn't share the big moment with me but we'd spent enough hours agonising over my future for me to know that she'd be right behind me in the move.

Dave Bowen picked me up an hour later and looked like he was enjoying himself. Weeks before he'd marked my card about Aldershot and when Kettering came in he was most insistent that I should take my time and not rush into anything I might regret later. Now he was about to drive me to Liverpool and oversee my transfer. It was a big deal for Northampton and a big break for me so everyone was happy. Dave has filled many positions at the County Ground including three spells as manager and his heart and soul are in the club. He'd been in charge for part of my time at Northampton and, looking back, I realise that he had total confidence in me. Mind you, he had a funny way of showing it because he had been the sort of boss who liked to have his players tearing each other's throats out. He loved to set one up against another by calling individuals into his office and getting them to slag off their team-mates. Then he'd use what they said in conversations with other players. As far as I was concerned, though, I reckoned he knew that Liverpool were interested and was convinced that I needed just one break to get going.

The four-hour journey seemed like eight, but Dave used the time to fill me in on the background to the deal and he offered advice based on his vast experience as a player with Arsenal. Bob Paisley had just taken over from the legendary Bill Shankly and was looking to strengthen his squad. His scouts had narrowed his options down to two players and it was his job to decide. Dave was claiming the credit for convincing them that I was the man for the job. No one needed to tell me what a great opportunity it was, but Dave talked about the Liverpool set-up and how I must expect to have to play my way into the first team squad. He warned me not to be greedy when talking terms, but he needn't have bothered – the way I was feeling by this time I would have signed a blank contract.

We arrived at the ground by lunch-time and ate in the canteen, although food was the last thing on my mind. I don't really know what I was expecting, certainly not the red-carpet treatment, but the place was as dead as a grave. We were shown into a back office to meet Bob Paisley – resplendent in one of those dreadful cardigans that were to become his trademark. To think I'd gone to the trouble of getting changed! The fee had been set at £60,000 – quite staggering in view of the fact that 40 miles down the road the chairman at Bury was still arguing with his manager over whether or not I was really worth £7,000. Obviously my hidden talent as a goalkeeper had added £53,000 to the fee overnight.

Then came the medical, and what a joke that turned out to be. Ten minutes with the club doctor who asked me whether I'd had any serious injuries and then tested my eyesight by asking if I could read from a simple chart on the wall. 'What chart?' I asked. 'That'll do nicely', he replied, and I was passed 100 per cent fit.

Seriously, though, anyone who thinks that clubs like Liverpool give their prospective signings anything more than a cursory glance are sadly mistaken. Perhaps if they did take their medical checks seriously many of the big money transfers that end up with the insurance assessors wouldn't go through in the first place. Needless to say, terms weren't a problem. Sixty pounds a week in the reserves, and four pounds for a win. Nobody mentioned the first team and I didn't like to ask. The club offered me a room in an hotel until I could get the family fixed up and that tied up the day's business ... or at least I thought it did. I later learned that Dave Bowen, wily as ever, had used the period during which I was sorting out the formalities to tap Bob Paisley about the prospect of sending a side down to Northampton to provide the opposition for his own testimonial. Bob agreed and a few months later we played there. I was captain for the night, the County Ground was fuller than it had been in years and Dave laughed all the way to the bank. When I see him these days I still pull his leg about that stroke – he made a lot more money than I did on the day.

That was all in the future, though, as the solitary photographer recorded the event for posterity and Bob Paisley obliged the local press with a quote about signing me as defensive cover. I was convinced he meant for Ray Clemence until he added, perhaps feeling his first statement was a little bare, that he also thought I could 'play a bit'. Now, 12 years later, I realise that this is a great compliment when it comes from Mr Paisley. For my part, I was still in a state of shock and could manage only a few words about what a fantastic opportunity it was and how Liverpool were one of the best teams in the country. The next thing I knew we were back in the car park and ready for the drive home. On impulse I dived into the Anfield souvenier shop and bought myself a 'Reds' scarf which was still draped proudly around my neck when I breezed into the hospital ward to visit Sue that evening.

Naturally she was delighted. The long spell in hospital was beginning to depress her but this was the tonic she needed: at last things were going to happen and we were on our way.

I got together with my new team-mates for a Central League game at Coventry the following evening. It was a strange atmosphere because, even with a club like Liverpool, there's something unreal about playing in the reserves. The stadium was empty and the game lacked the fierce competitive edge that exists only in first team games regardless of the standard. We ran out easy 5-1 winners but, apart from the result, there was nothing really memorable about the game.

My education in the ways of Liverpool Football Club began 24 hours later when I reported to Anfield for the first time. There must have been 60 players on the staff in those days – a staggering number compared with Northampton – and each morning we were ferried by coach from the stadium to the club's training ground at Melwood. Some days it was three to a seat or standing room only and I can tell you, if the journey there was uncomfortable then the ride back, with 60 filthy, sweaty bodies piled like cattle in a truck going to market, was one of the most unpleasant experiences imaginable. At Northampton there had been no problem. There were never more than a dozen or so players and we drove to the training field in a battered old van with me at the wheel. That way I was always guaranteed a seat.

The first thing I noticed about training at Liverpool was the difference in methods. At Northampton, the emphasis had been on stamina and this had always meant a lot of running. At Liverpool, though, the routine was very different and rarely varied. We usually began with a leisurely but thorough warm-up, followed by a series of sprints. Then in no time at all we were into a series of five-a-sides, each taken very seriously. The amount of time we spent with the ball was exhilarating. Right from the start I felt I had joined a club where a certain level of ability and fitness was taken as read. The coaching staff saw it as their job to develop that talent and refine it – get them used to the so-called 'Liverpool way' if you like.

The Gospel according to Liverpool had been handed down to Bob Paisley by Bill Shankly via the famous 'boot room' think tank and I remember how Bob came across as something of an odd character to a newcomer. He had an office overlooking the training field at Melwood and would stand for hours peering out of the window as Ronnie Moran and Joe Fagan put the players through their paces. I thought it was his way of keeping his finger on the pulse, never missing a trick, but I soon discovered that underneath this same window was the room's only radiator. I could have sympathised had it not been for the fact that one of the golden rules at Liverpool was no tracksuits during training whatever the weather and believe me it could get pretty cold at Melwood! Eventually, almost reluctantly, the boss would make his way down to the touchline and watch the practice match. On the face of it he seemed detached, daydreaming almost, but in reality he was taking everything in.

I remember one particular day shortly after I arrived at the club. He pulled me to one side as we trooped off the practice pitch and in the space of a few minutes changed my whole approach to the defensive game. Throughout my professional career, whenever I'd played at full-back I'd been used to 'showing' the winger the touchline and encouraging him to try to beat me down the outside. They usually did, but in theory I felt I had enough pace to see off most of them on the run and was convinced that even down by the corner flag the worst I could do would be to concede a corner. Bob wanted me to change my approach completely and force the attacker inside. That way, he reasoned, the winger would be operating in foreign territory, on his wrong foot and facing the central defenders and goalkeeper head on. We would therefore have a much better chance of dispossessing him and breaking the attack down.

Bob's theory was simplicity itself, yet it was something I had never even thought of. I started putting his idea into practice and soon realised how effective it could be. Even if I didn't make so many spectacular tackles, I realised that I was driving my opponent into the most heavily populated area of the field. His job was to get crosses over and by forcing him inside I was rendering him ineffective. The scheme was brilliant but Bob just wandered away leaving me with the clear notion that these sort of tactical ideas came to him at any hour of the day or night.

I joined Liverpool during a period of transition. Bill Shankly had left a solid set-up but Bob Paisley realised that some of the players were nearing the end of their careers and changes would have to be made. At 23 I had time on my side. I'd been given the chance to join the squad. It was up to me now to prove that I could be more than an occasional first-team player and I was determined to lose that 'utility player' tag once and for all.

The dressing-room in those days accommodated some of

the greatest names in the game. Spending each day in the company of people like Tommy Smith, Emlyn Hughes and Kevin Keegan could be quite daunting. As the new boy, I looked and listened but said very little during the early weeks. I was amazed how attitudes differed. There were those players who simply loved training and put everything into it and alongside them were lads like Alec Lindsey – at the time an England full-back – who would do anything to avoid work. The sprints were his pet hate and he'd pull any trick in the book to avoid them. He was one of the few lads in the squad who smoked and we'd often have to cover for him while he nipped round the back of the groundsman's hut for a crafty drag. I swear he kept a packet of five inside his jock-strap.

Emlyn was another player who knew how to work the system. To the great British public he's a hero, the lad from next door who made it to the top. At Liverpool it wasn't quite like that. Emlyn was one of the meanest men I'd ever met and if that wasn't bad enough, he was also one of those irritating know-alls. In fact he's on television so much these days I'm surprised he hasn't yet made it on to *Mastermind*, but then again perhaps he's got too many specialist subjects! Then of course there was Kevin Keegan, or KK as he was known around the club. He was a major influence in the dressing-room even then but his star was destined to burn brighter still.

From the very beginning I counted myself lucky that my dressing-room peg was next to that of Ian Callaghan. Cally was well over 30 by that time but still fending off all comers for his number 11 shirt, so much so that he was still to win his final England cap. I was delighted to be one of the six Liverpool players to share the experience with him when he was 35 years old. His enthusiasm for the game was unbelievable and his attitude an example to everyone. Day after day he'd turn up for training and never give less than 100 per cent. To him, football was a simple game to be enjoyed to the full and it was obvious that he counted himself fortunate to be earning his living from something he loved and would gladly have done for nothing. Cally was my example in those early days and even now I believe that it is mainly because I adopted a similiar attitude in my work that I have managed to keep in such good shape for so long.

It is interesting to note that some of the other lads who weren't so keen on those cold winter mornings departed for the soft comfort of much easier yet less fulfilling working environments many seasons ago. Indeed with some of them, their slack attitude to training was a reflection of their approach to life in general, and once they slipped out of football they found their existence away from the game even more difficult to adjust to. Even today when I'm coaching youngsters or talking to apprentices I try to drill into them the fact that they cannot hope to get to the top or stay there for a reasonable period on ability alone. The heart has to be there too and that means driving the body to its limits even during the early years when fitness comes so easily. It's like money in the bank later in life because it is the players who are dedicated enough to do this in their youth that enjoy playing on well into their 30s.

7
Life at The Kop

The one thing that intrigues every football fan in the country is the secret of Liverpool's remarkable run of success. Everyone seems convinced that there is one vital ingredient that has helped the club achieve almost 15 years of dominance in England and Europe. I hate to be the one to destroy the myth, but, having been a part of the Anfield set-up for more than a decade, I'm forced to admit that there is no one element I can put my finger on and say 'that makes Liverpool different from the rest'. Apart, of course, from the fact that the club has always had some very good players.

Indeed, sometimes I wonder myself just why we achieved so much because the set-up behind the scenes resembled that of any number of clubs. At Anfield everything is very basic and down-to-earth. The players are just like any bunch of working-class lads in a factory ... although the overalls do tend to have designer labels. They have their rows and occasionally their punch-ups, but generally as a group they get along very well. You don't get to Liverpool unless you've proved you can do the job and everyone is determined to do their best for the club. Training, as I've mentioned elsewhere, places great emphasis on ball skills, but perhaps more surprisingly it never varies, week-in week-out the routine is exactly the same. It's a repetitive diet that has brought the club consistent success but I can't help wondering what the atmosphere would have been like had they not been so successful. I'm sure would have been among the first to complain that it was monotonous.

In my view, any rigid routine becomes boring after a time and Liverpool's training schedule was no exception. Successive managers have stuck with it, but no one has ever really questioned why. I for one would have preferred more variety and it will be interesting to see whether Kenny Dalglish has the courage to break the mould and introduce new methods – somehow I doubt it because as long as the side keeps winning all the powerful voices in the famous 'boot-room' will be able to claim without fear of contradiction that the results on the field fully justify the system. I'd go even further and suggest that something as simple as superstition could be at the heart of the matter. I reckon some of the coaches fear that a change in the training pattern could burst the Anfield bubble. It's a very old-fashioned club in many respects.

Another myth I must explode is the image the fans have of a top player's lifestyle. Most people only see them from the terraces on a Saturday or read about them on the back pages of their dailies ... occasionally other pages if you happen to play for Arsenal! The general idea is that they lead a cosseted existence with the club looking after their every need from breakfast-time through to bed-time; well sadly, nothing could be further from the truth. And as for that other popular belief that they live the sort of lives enjoyed by pop singers and film stars, well again I'm sorry to disappoint you – and me for that matter – because that's not true either. As I said before, footballers are mostly just working-class lads with a lifestyle to match – plain and simple. Take food for instance. We all remember the Leeds United side of the late 1960s when Don Revie had his players so wrapped up in cotton wool that he regularly checked up on their home lives and even went so far as to send their wives shopping lists and diet sheets to ensure they bought the right things. Well, I can assure you that certainly wasn't the Anfield way.

When I first joined Liverpool Sue and the children were still in Northampton, so the club fixed me up with an hotel room, but the place was a disaster. I made up my mind to move out the night I discovered that I'd got a couple of rats for room-mates. Instead I moved into digs with a couple of the apprentices whose enterprising landlady had got to hear of my plight and passed word that she had a third bed available. That third bed turned out to be a 'put-you-up' in a freezing cold bedroom over the garage, not quite the ideal environment for a player expected to play out of his skin each week and force his way into the first team. I remember a particular night when one of the youngsters was so cold he had to throw his overcoat over the bed to keep warm. I nipped downstairs to ask Mrs T. if she could spare him an extra blanket. She was sitting in the front room with a couple of visitors and flashed me the filthiest look. 'It's not an overcoat, it's an eiderdown', she snapped. 'Well, he's got his foot caught in the pocket', I replied. If the accommodation was spartan then the food had to be sampled to be believed. It was a case of chips with everything including, one day, black pudding. Mrs T. was into carbohydrate-loading years before the rest of the world started running marathons!

At Liverpool, as long as you were fit, the club didn't take a lot of interest in what you ate during the week, and while that may have been all right for someone like me, because Sue made sure I got a balanced diet with lots of green vegetables, I did wonder about some of the single lads. Too many of them were overly fond of the old take-aways and hamburgers. Food of a very different kind could pose a problem too for the big money signings who find themselves living in one of Liverpool's top hotels until they get themselves fixed up. As a rule the club will foot the bill for up to six months and for those players temptation is around 24 hours of the day.

Everyone likes to stay in a good hotel from time to time, but how many of you would fancy the idea permanently?

You can get too much of a good thing as Dolly Parton's husband used to say. I remember my old Liverpool team-mate Ray Clemence complaining about the problems of living in an hotel just a few months after he joined Spurs. For a start you're in a strange city and your new team-mates all have their own lives to lead. Training occupies only a couple of hours of the day and boredom sets in for the remainder. Eating and drinking help to fill in the time and the next thing you know you're over your playing weight and struggling. Putting on a few pounds is so easy and it's amazing what an effect the surplus can have on your game.

I suppose in many respects I was lucky. I wasn't a big money signing so I didn't get the five-star treatment and because I'd never lived away from home before I was anxious to get my family up to Merseyside as quickly as possible. That, combined with Mrs T.'s cooking, was the very incentive I needed and within a couple of months I was renting a house from Peter Spiring, who had just been transferred away from the club.

I was married by the time I was 20, so I've known a stable family background throughout my football career but I sometimes wonder how some of the other lads get on. At one time it was the norm for footballers to marry early and I remember how Matt Busby used to pray that George Best would get himself hitched. He was convinced that a wife could keep him on the rails. Times have changed, though, and nowadays many players stay single well into their careers. Few remain in digs, most buy their own flats or houses.

The single life for a footballer with no interests outside the game is laden with temptation and too many players fall into the trap. I suppose the working pattern creates a lot of the problems because on a typical mid-week day they report to the ground for training at ten o'clock and are back, showered and changed by one o'clock, leaving an awful lot of time on their hands. There's no doubt that some of the lads do get in with the wrong crowd and when they do they're asking for trouble, because the clubs and pubs of Liverpool are teaming with people just itching to have a go and it only takes that one drink too many or a careless comment delivered on the spur of the moment for trouble to start. Discipline at Liverpool has been excellent over the years, but even at Anfield there have been one or two embarrassing incidents that should never have been allowed to happen. The players involved know only too well what they did wrong and a couple of them ended up paying the ultimate price and being transferred.

Liverpool is a proud club and any breaches of discipline are frowned upon. On the odd occasions when there have been lapses the club has always said very little publicly, but privately the individuals have been left under no illusions that they have let themselves and the club down. I don't know whether there are more problems now than there were a few years ago, but what I did become increasingly aware of towards the end of my Liverpool career was a steady erosion of the intimate team spirit that had previously been such a strong point within the club.

For a long time during my Liverpool days we used to have lunch at Anfield, but the arrival of David Hodgson – a £400,000 signing from Middlesbrough – apparently stretched the purse strings so much that the club decided to scrap the meals as an economy measure. The management claimed that by getting rid of them they could save £50,000 a year but sadly they never gave a moment's thought to the effects of the measure on the collective spirit of its players. Naturally, Hodgy took some good-natured ribbing over the loss of the meals, but that aside, I honestly believe that it was a great mistake to do away with them. The food itself was nothing special – it was brought in daily from a local catering firm – but that lunch-time get-together helped to foster a great atmosphere within the club.

We always ate in the players' lounge at tables for six and

an apprentice could find himself passing the salt to Tommy Smith. That would probably be the only thing he ever got to pass to Tommy but never mind, it helped to make the youngsters feel as much a part of the set-up as the rest of us. The lunches kept the lads together for an extra hour or so and the chat wasn't always about football ... there was always time for our other favourites like birds, booze and Einstein's theory of relativity. Seriously, though, I felt we all knew each other a lot better in those days.

It was always a great way to test out the new lads and I remember when Alan Kennedy signed from Newcastle, some months after I'd joined the club. No one knew very much about him or his character, but one or two of the lads had heard that he was a bit short of the 'grey matter'. They decided to put him to the test and as we got back from training on his first morning one of the boys slipped a piece of paper to the girl on reception ... a message for Alan. Alan went into lunch and the girl gave him the note which said: 'Urgent – ring 430-9009 – Mr C. Lyon wants to talk to you about a personal appearance'.

Alan was grinning from ear to ear, in the big time at last, yet trying to appear like 'Joe Cool'. Most of the other players were in on the joke and trying desperately to keep straight faces. Alan didn't rush, but it was clear he was looking for the phone. One of the lads pointed out the pay phone in the corner and he ambled across, trying for all the world to look as though he'd been talking to big time agents every day of the week at Newcastle. As he dialled the number the other lads started to creep up behind him and by the time he got through there must have been 20 of us all in on the joke and earwigging on the conversation.

'Knowsley', a lady's voice answered.

'Mr Lyon, please', asked Alan ... Knowsley? Must be the name of the agency. They probably deal with all the big money stars so no wonder the other lads haven't heard of them!

Pause.

'Mr C. Lyon?'. He looked puzzled.

There was a longer pause and the penny began to drop. He hung up and turned: 'You b......!'. The rest was lost as the other guys fell about. Alan had been given the number of the Knowsley Safari Park and had been given short shrift by the girl on the other end who had heard the joke a hundred times before. A silly little stunt I know, but we found out more about Alan's sense of humour and ability to take a joke in those few mintues than in a week on the training field at Melwood.

To create that sort of atmosphere you have to have the right environment and latterly, without the traditional lunch-time get-together, that feeling was missing. Instead the lads came back from training, showered and changed and then went their separate ways. Surprising though it may seem, there were some players about whom I knew nothing even after they'd been at the club for a couple of seasons. They would come in and do their work and then go off on their own after training. I hadn't the first clue about how they spent their spare time.

Even more worrying is the little amount of attention even a big club like Liverpool paid to the welfare of its staff. There was an excellent pension scheme there I admit, but that's where the club believed its responsibility ended. Young stars were paid vast amounts of money on the strength of their football ability but no one offered them any sort of advice about what they should do with it. There were plenty of people around who would help the lads spend their cash but nobody specifically employed by the club to tell them how to look after it. Everyone knows that the big money is supposed to compensate for the fact that a career in football is a short one, but it needs a sound financial mind and a respected personality to get that fact across to a kid who has just made it rich and can't wait to splash out on his first leather suit.

There are players at Liverpool who have done stupid

things with their money. One had to knock £10,000 off the selling price of his house because he had paid too much for it in the first place and another – just 21 – has splashed out on a sports car that costs him almost £300 a quarter just to insure. I am lucky because I spent enough years struggling to make ends meet on Fourth Division wages to prevent me from being tempted to take the big money for granted. I've always looked after my cash and sought good, independent advice about what to do with it. Some of the other lads who've never had to struggle in the same way seem to take the money as a matter of course. They don't understand, and no one bothers to remind them, that the fat wage packets will be there only for as long as they're playing and, even if they have an exceptional run, maintaining top form and steering clear of injuries, that won't be much after they turn 35.

Only the fortunate few stay in the game as either coaches or managers – 95 per cent of players who make a career out of professional football have to find themselves a second career when they stop playing, and at 35 they're competing for jobs with people who can have up to 19 years' start on them. Most players at one time or another talk glibly about moving into coaching or management at the end of their playing days, but few take into account the fact that there are 92 Football League clubs, each with at least 16 players, and of those 16 players the majority believe they have something to offer the game once they hang up their boots. The facts are there for anyone to see. Only a fraction of the players who sign on as professionals – the most successful of them included – can expect to find a niche once they have finished playing. Players like Kevin Keegan who earn enough from the game to see them through the rest of their lives are few and far between. The vast majority leave the game with perhaps a few bob in the bank from a testimonial and a well-known name to trade off.

I think it would make good sense for each club or group of clubs to employ a full-time personnel officer to advise young players, a person who would put the star players in touch with the right people to handle their investments, convince the youngsters about the need to continue their studies and help those apprentices who sadly don't make the grade to come to terms with the fact and get themselves fixed up with a career outside the game. It is a simple enough idea, and a good way for the clubs to improve their image as employers, but I'm sure it will never happen because, after all, they're only players, and as long as they are doing a good job on the park that's all that really matters.

Critics claim that football has lived for too long in an monetary wonderland untouched by the cold reality of the present economic climate. Well, while that may be true of some clubs, Liverpool is a definite exception – success on the field there has never been reflected in the way players are treated off it. At Anfield, everything was done on a tight budget from our travel and accommodation at away games through to the light bulbs in the club offices – they were all swapped down from 100 watts to 60 watts to save on the electricity bill once the European ban took effect!

When I first arrived at the club we used to travel to most away games by train and it suited the players down to the ground. There was plenty of room to stretch out and a nice meal and a few drinks on the way home to wind down after the match. Three seasons ago, though, some financial wizard worked out that it was too expensive and the directors decided that the 'age of the train' had passed. Instead they hired a coach and from that moment on we enjoyed the delights of touring Britain's motorway system.

When the news was first announced the lads were up in arms and protests were long and loud. Needless to say our complaints fell on deaf ears and on the following Friday we boarded the bus for a trip to London. Everyone moaned a bit as the packed lunches were handed around but generally the trip down the M6 was uneventful. The problems started on the M1, where we ran into our first set of roadworks just on a stretch where the railway runs alongside the road. There we were, windows steamed up and tempers to match, as express after express sped past. In the end – much to the annoyance of the driver – Terry McDermott led the boys in an impromptu rendition of Jimmy Savile's favourite ditty.

Once the idea of the coach had been reluctantly accepted, the club took its economy drive a step further by cutting out the post-match meals. Well, to be strictly accurate I tell a lie because for a while, for some bizarre reason, we continued to stop at an hotel in North Yorkshire whenever we played Newcastle. At first, I suspected this was just a one-off to celebrate our return to civilisation but when even that stopover was cancelled I realised that it been merely an oversight. After that, following every away game the team coach would pull up in regal splendour outside a fish and chip shop close to the ground and one of the lads would be detailed to pick up the box of suppers ordered over the phone a few minutes earlier. Perhaps I should prepare a guide to the fish and chip shops of the Football League.

In the old days we used to spend the Friday night before each home game locked away from the world in a Cheshire hotel. The idea was to have an early meal together and a chat about the next day's game and then go off to bed with a glass of milk for a good night's sleep. Most of the players had babies at home in those days, so Friday night away was an important part of the preparation because it guaranteed a settled night's sleep. Needless to say the axe fell here too, but by the time it did there were few complaints. Most of the lads agreed that they preferred to spend Friday nights at home with the family.

Traditionally on match days the Liverpool players meet at an hotel around 11.00 am and have an early lunch. The routine – like the training – never varies. There's a choice of steak, chicken or fish accompanied by tea and toast and a few nervous jokes. The day's game is seldom discussed and the lads reckon to be finished about ten minutes after they've started. Then it's everyone into the TV lounge for the football previews and another chance to see just how well they played the week before! The exception to this pre-match tradition is Craig Johnston, who's into the healthy eating kick. He brings his own bag of nuts and muesli with him.

The coach arrives at Anfield about 1.45 and then it's down to the business of preparing for the game. Again, there are no hard and fast rules about being in the dressing-room at a certain time but most players like to be safely shut away an hour before kick-off. I became particularly rigid about this as I got older because I believe it becomes increasingly important to get mentally prepared for the game. Not everyone agrees with me, though, and at Liverpool some of the younger lads tend to hang around with their friends in the players' lounge and the punters in the team sit glued to the racing until the last possible minute.

By and large there's no pressure from the management, although I can remember one period during Bob Paisley's reign as manager when the results weren't going our way and for some reason the boss decided the TV racing was to blame. We were told in no uncertain terms that we must be in the dressing-room by two o'clock and for the betting lads this was a devastating blow because the 2.15 was often the big race of the day. On reflection, the decision must have hurt Bob as much as it did Smithy and the other boys because he was as big a gambling man as any of them, but he stuck to his word and for the next three weeks we were in the dressing-room by two o'clock and no messing. Coincidentally, the results picked up and Bob was walking around with the air of a man who had masterminded the tactical breakthrough of the century.

The next Saturday we were all getting changed as usual when the boss popped his head around the door. 'Tommy, let us know who wins the 2.15 will you?'. It was Bob's way of letting us know that the heat was off.

There was another occasion a few seasons later. We were 3-0 up at half-time and playing the other team off the park. Alan Hansen was having a blinder and as we were coming down the tunnel Bob was waiting at the dressing-room door grinning broadly. I was right behind Alan as we reached the boss and suddenly Bob threw an arm around the lad's shoulder. I was thinking that the gesture might be just a touch premature in view of the fact that there were another 45 minutes to play when I heard Bob say: 'It won you know!'. Suddenly, Alan was jumping up and down too and it turned out that Bob was talking about the 3.30. Apparently Alan had given him a tip and the boss had put his shirt on the horse. He must have slipped away from the directors' box at the appropriate moment and nipped into the players' lounge to watch the race. He was delighted with the result and seemed to be reasonably happy too with the way the game was going!

While I am writing about the dressing-room I might as well touch on some of those much talked-about pre-match superstitions we're all supposed to have. I've never really got involved myself, but there was one cup run a few seasons ago when I pulled on a sock before the third round game and discovered a hole in it. I played with the hole, we won the tie and I went through the entire cup run cutting a hole in one of my socks for luck. I've never let on before, though, because in view of the way Liverpool watch the pennies I was worried that someone might order me to buy a new set.

Mark Lawrenson is another player with an expensive pre-match habit. He contrives to snap his bootlaces before tying them up. I'm not sure the boss has twigged yet, but if he does I reckon Mark will be told to provide his own.

Bruce Grobbelaar – naturally – has the wildest ritual of the lot. He has to switch off the dressing-room light by kicking a football at it. He starts at two o'clock and will not allow himself to throw the ball. Some weeks everything is fine, he knocks the light off at the first or second attempt and settles down. On the other hand I've been there when it has got to within ten minutes of the kick-off and he has still not managed to do it. The boss might be there waiting for a final word and the boys will be yelling at Bruce to change the rules or call it a day, but no, the light has to go out or Bruce won't!

Team-talks at Liverpool were never the serious business many people might think. They generally took place on a Friday and seldom dealt in any depth with the opposition. The staff would talk about our strengths and we would concentrate on the way we were going to play the next day and not on what the opposition might do. I soon discovered on joining the club that tactics didn't really figure on Bob Paisley's list of priorities. He believed much more in assembling the right blend of players and then allowing them freedom of expression on the park. Nevertheless he did go through the motions with a weekly team-talk and these were some of the funniest episodes in the Anfield week.

I remember as a new boy looking forward to my first Friday team meeting with some anticipation, so imagine my surprise when Tommy Smith sat down a few chairs away, put his feet up and unfolded his copy of the *Sporting Life*. I was waiting for the sparks to fly but no, Bob just got on with his chat and left Smithy to get on with picking the next day's winners. Ten minutes into the talk and the boss was droning on and Tommy was deeply engrossed in the Haydock card. 'Now you've got to keep it tight at the back tomorrow because this team likes to punk it', said the boss. Quick as a flash, Tommy dropped the paper on to his lap. 'What the f … hell does "punk it" mean?' he called out. 'Punk it Tommy, you know, punk it'. Bob was making great, sweeping gestures with his arm, leaving no one in any doubt about what he meant, but Smithy was playing dumb and the rest of the lads were enjoying every minute of it. The boss tried all sorts of tricks to get his message across before he finally twigged that Tommy was taking the mickey, and the meeting broke up in pandemonium. Next day, though, everyone remembered the message – the back four was as secure as Fort Knox and the other team went home empty-handed.

There was another occasion just before an important European Cup tie when Bob turned to me during the team meeting: 'Right Phil, you'll have to watch yourself with this winger tonight. He's not quick but he's nippy'. He brought the house down.

The Liverpool philosophy is simple, and is based on total belief. Maybe that has been the important key to Liverpool's consistency. We were taught to go out there, play our own game and fear no one. Off the field, too, for their own reasons, the management likes to keep it simple. A simple lifestyle for a group of simple fellows – maybe that's what kept us hungry.

8
It's All About Players

I've played either alongside or against some of the greatest names in football. Generally my team-mates have more than lived up to their reputations, but as far as the opponents are concerned it has often been a very different matter – some of the unlikeliest players have ended up giving me the most trouble as a full-back.

In the early days, when I was making my way at Northampton, the name Len Glover used to strike fear in my heart. Because Leicester was just a stone's throw away, we would often end up playing our First Division neighbours in pre-season friendlies. As I remember they had a reasonable side in those days, and Len Glover was one of the jewels in their crown, a quick, jinking winger who could take on either full-back on either side. On one hand I would look forward to playing against him but on the other I would have nightmares at night in case he made a fool of me.

I'd like to be able to boast that the young pretender taught the old guy one or two tricks, but I'm afraid that only ever really happens in the movies. Len would twist me inside out mercilessly for 80 minutes of the game and I would go back into the Northampton dressing-room congratulating myself for getting the better of him a couple of times in the match. In my opinion Len was underrated. He made almost 250 appearances on Leicester's left wing between 1967 and 1975 yet never achieved international honours. He is someone I will always remember from those early years because although it may not have seemed so at the time, I'm sure he helped me to become a wiser, less impetuous player. Funnily enough, there seemed to be a talented and genuinely honest sort of pro at most clubs in the late '60s and early '70s, but today I'm afraid they are something of a dying breed.

Another player who has plagued me over the years is certainly talented but could never be described as a model pro – in fact he'd probably try to sue me if I ever dared to suggest he was! John Robertson, Nottingham Forest's Scottish international, was slow, overweight and at times abusive but, hand on heart, I have to admit that he probably gave me more problems during my life at the Kop than any other winger. Robbo was a talker, the sort of player who loved to try to break your concentration during the crucial periods of a game. I saw a lot of him during my Liverpool days because either we were playing Forest in vital matches or I would be lining up against him at international level.

John Robertson had two great talents. The first was his ability to take the ball past the full-back, and his second, and far more important attribute was his common sense. Once John gets past his man he gets his cross in. There is no room for fancy antics with him, he is truly an unselfish player who thinks only in terms of his duty to the team. Once Robbo is past you, there is never a second chance because he won't hang on to the ball long enough. Your only hope is to get a successful tackle in first otherwise all you will see is his big, fat bum as he shapes to chip a perfect cross to the far post.

At Anfield we used to liken matches against Forest to games of chess, because as opponents they were always so patient, prepared to play negative football yet at the same time waiting to seize on any mistake we might make. Consequently, games between our two sides were rarely classics and Robbo was never short of a word or two about the standard of the football. Just last season, I met up with him again before one of my last appearances in a Liverpool shirt. This time the occasion was a Central League fixture at the City Ground and as I walked towards the players' entrance I caught sight of John, leaning against the door, cigarette in hand, and we exchanged a few words. Later, out on the pitch, he couldn't resist trying to draw me into conversation by having a go at other players on the park, even though it was only a reserve game.

If Robbo was bad, though, the Welsh international winger Leighton James was a whole lot worse. In many ways he was easier to handle as a player because he couldn't resist trying to make a monkey of you every time he got the ball, regardless of the position. The early cross was something that never seemed to enter his head. He just loved taking players on and when things were going his way he was one of the best in the business. However, the main problem with Leighton was that he was easily put off his game and could lose heart after the most trifling of setbacks, and that is when the tantrums would start. He would tear into the other players. 'Look at him, who does he think he is?' or 'This ref's got it in for me, never gives me a break!'. Then he would start baiting the referee, diving as soon as anyone went near him and then remonstrating with the ref when he failed to give a free kick. Inevitably, the book would come out eventually and Leighton's name would go into it. Then I always knew that the bulk of my afternoon's defensive work would be over, because Leighton would be completely demoralised and play out the rest of the afternoon sulking on the wing.

It was a shame really because he was a good player, but I think his temperament prevented him from ever realising his full potential. He exploded on to the scene with Burnley and enjoyed some success at Derby during Dave Mackay's reign, but even then his approach to the game was his worst enemy. Later, as he moved on from club to club, never really settling anywhere, he offered only brief flashes of the talent that should have ensured him a place in

Welsh football's hall of fame. Instead he ended up being nicknamed the 'Mavis Riley' of the First Division.

There was nothing so soft about another winger who courted trouble wherever he played. I'm talking about West Bromwich Albion's Scottish international Willie Johnstone, who, besides the shameful disgrace of being caught up in the Scottish squad's drug-taking scandal during the 1978 World Cup finals in Argentina, was also notorious for having one of the worst disciplinary records in the Football League. If Willie fancied his chance on the day he had the ability to turn you inside out, and sometimes I've seen him try to take the ball around the same player twice, just for the hell of it!

Willie had tremendous ability, he was skilful and quick and an excellent crosser of the ball, but so easily riled when things weren't going too well. Then he became an animal. He would make wild lunges at you, not caring whether he caught you or the ball, and his elbows would be everywhere. Willie was also a great one for the verbals – particularly when he had beaten an opponent – and would wind them up until they could take no more and punches were exchanged. More often than not, though, it would be Willie who would find himself either in the referee's book or on the lonely walk back to the tunnel because if ever a man had a reputation as one of football's bad boys, it was him, and the referees were always on the look-out for trouble.

At Anfield, Tommy Smith, Jimmy Case and Graeme Souness provided much of the steel in the hearts of our successful sides. Smithy's reputation as a hard man was well known the world over, but all too often during the pre-match build-up the word 'bad' was substituted for 'hard' and Tommy became a target for the opposition's self-styled tough guy. Naturally for a tough Liverpudlian, Smithy was always more than up to the challenge and even viewed from a few yards away some of his tackles were awesome. Sadly, Tommy is now having to pay the price for his endeavours and only another series of major knee operations looks likely to save him from spending his life on pain-killing drugs.

You could fill a book with stories about Tommy Smith, but we all have our favourites. I'll never forget a trip behind the Iron Curtain for the second leg of a European Cup tie. We had played well at Anfield and were taking a two-goal lead with us for the return match, and everyone was confident that we would get a result. From the first whistle, though, it was obvious that we were playing a very different side. They came at us in wave after relentless wave and 20 minutes into the match had levelled the scores and were running us ragged. I was convinced that they must have been on drugs the way they were performing, it was uncanny. All their main plays were being engineered by the man Tommy was supposed to be marking.

We were fighting for our lives out there and Tommy was chasing his man all over the field. Midway through the half Tommy's man had skinned him yet again and only a full-stretch fingertip save from Ray Clemence had kept the scores level. As we lined up for the corner one of the lads shouted across to Tommy: 'Smithy, hit him for Christ's sake!'. The 'iron man' grimaced, his shirt steaming in the bitterly cold night air: 'Hit him? I can't get f...... near enough!'.

Fortunately for us all the effects of whatever the Poles had been taking to improve their performance wore off rapidly after the interval and we were able to get back into the game and snatch a result with a late goal.

Graeme Souness was always a far more cultured player than most, but he had a fearsome competitive streak which would occasionally see him lose control in the most public of fashions. His much publicised 'frustration foul' while captaining Scotland is a classic example, but what few people realise is that Graeme's nationalistic pride is a major motivating factor in his game. At Anfield, the rivalry between the English lads and the Scots was always apparent and most of us treated it as little more than a bit of harmless fun that helped make it easier to choose the teams for a five-a-side game. Graeme, though, took a different attitude, treating practice games almost as seriously as full-blown internationals and on the odd occasion things got out of hand with players picking up needless injuries at Melwood.

My relationship with Graeme was generally very good, but one morning he was in a particularly bad mood and seemed hell-bent on needling me. He was pushing and shoving, tapping my ankles and generally making a nuisance of himself until finally I snapped. The next thing I knew we were shaping up to each other and Ronnie Moran and a couple of other lads had to pull us apart. It was over and done with in a flash, and neither Graeme nor I bore any grudges, but with hard men like that facing up to you on the training field, who needs to be worried about opponents with reputations on a Saturday?

Off the field, Graeme was as nice a bloke as you could wish to meet with a taste for gold jewellery *á la* Ron Atkinson, expensive clothes and even a gold American Express card. He was at the centre of a group of players who believed that their success as footballers had earned them the right to the good things in life.

Emlyn Hughes was another in this category, but unlike Graeme he always thought that his money should be kept well out of sight. One occasion I'll never forget came during Liverpool's trip to London for the 1977 FA Cup final against Manchester United. We got to the team's hotel just around the corner from Harrods on the night before the game and when he unpacked his bag Emlyn discovered to his horror that he'd forgotten to pack a pair of shoes to go with his match day suit. Everyone was in fits because stories of Emlyn's meanness were legendary at the club and the prospect of him having to start his match day preparations with the purchase of a new pair of shoes seemed bound to put him in a great frame of mind for the game.

Next morning, though, he allowed himself to be pointed in the direction of Harrods for his shopping trip. Half an hour later he was back, complaining that he couldn't find anything that he liked for less than £40 and that there was no way he was going to waste that sort of money when he'd got a perfectly good pair back at home. No one really took him seriously until the time came to leave for Wembley and Emlyn appeared in the lobby dressed in an immaculate grey suit like the rest of us, but wearing a pair of red training shoes instead of conventional footwear!

Meanness is one thing, but being careful is something else. I know that I belong to the latter school but Kevin Keegan was perhaps the best example of this philosophy. His roots in the game couldn't have been more humble but he worked hard at improving himself, and when Bill Shankly brought him to Liverpool he systematically set about training himself into England's most complete all-round performer. Kevin never made any secret of the fact that he was determined to use the game to get rich and ensure his future, but at the same time he seldom shirked his responsibilities and never let the team down on a Saturday.

Occasionally it did look as though the management enforced one set of rules and regulations for the first team squad and another for Kevin Keegan – much the same as I suspect they did in later years with Kenny Dalglish – and this usually meant that K.K. had no trouble in getting the odd day off when he wanted to make a bit on the side by opening a supermarket. Generally, though, he mucked in with the rest of us when it came to football but kept himself very much to himself once his training and playing responsibilities were out of the way.

He took his family to live near Mold, less than an hour from Merseyside yet in the heart of the fervently nationalist area of North Wales. For a long time his family were treated appallingly by the locals, who vandalised their house and then in one particularly sick incident attacked his daughter's pet pony. Yet throughout that whole sorry experience, Kevin never moaned, showing instead the sort of gritty, single-minded determination that was to prove one of the hallmarks of his outstanding career.

The public got their first indication of Kevin's determination when in early 1977, with his contract drawing to a close, he announced that he would be leaving Anfield at the end of the season to pursue his career abroad. He was the first big star since the early 1960s to seek his fortune overseas and with Liverpool on the verge of scaling new heights at club level, few could believe that Keegan needed a new challenge at that time. Club officials, team-mates and the press were at their most persuasive, but Kevin wouldn't budge. He bowed out on a glorious Rome evening in May 1977 when Liverpool beat Borussia Moënchengladbach by three goals to one to take the European Cup for the first time. He started the next season in West Germany with S.V. Hamburg.

I've always felt that we played above ourselves that night in Rome thanks to the added significance of K.K.'s impending departure. Although Bob Paisley was well and truly in charge, I think many of the older players saw it as the start of the break-up of the team that Bill Shankly had built. Kevin might have been expected to have stayed around somewhat longer than one or two of the other lads but nevertheless he had decided to go and we were determined that he should have the best possible send-off. Kevin went on to achieve new goals in Europe, showing a determination to adapt to the West German lifestyle and to get on well with his new team-mates, yet in many ways while he was there the ghost of Liverpool remained to haunt him. For some reason we always pulled out that little bit extra whenever Hamburg provided the opposition. Something would stir as we sat in the dressing-room preparing for the game and on the field we couldn't seem to do anything wrong. Particularly memorable was the 6-1 drubbing we handed out in the final of the European Super Cup.

Kevin went on to show his resolution to put his financial future and the happiness of his family before his football sentiments on two other occasions, the first when he surprisingly returned to England at the height of his European career, and then later when he retired from Newcastle and turned his back on the game, steadfastly refusing to be tempted back despite a whole string of offers. Kevin Keegan was never a great player in my view, but he achieved more than almost anyone from his generation because he woke up to the potential of the game sooner than many better players around him and, more importantly, he was prepared to work as hard as was necessary to achieve his ambitions. I have no intention of knocking him for that.

Terry Venables is a managerial Kevin Keegan, in the sense that he developed a keen perception of what the game could offer him at a fairly early stage in his career and has pursued his ambitions with determination. Terry has another much sought-after attribute: charisma. It is his charisma and natural flair that have enabled him to flourish in one of soccer's most partisan cities and to succeed where so many top names have failed. Venables is arguably the world game's hottest managerial property. Look at the way the directors of some top English clubs made fools of themselves in public as they rushed to try to tempt him back to this country. In the end he decided on another season in Spain but you can bet that his decision was based on the fact that he feels he still has something to achieve at Barcelona, and that at no time did sentiment come into his thinking process. When the time is right he will move on to a new challenge, and without regrets, but he'll move when he wants to not at anyone else's bidding.

I had some dealings with Terry Venables when I was an England player and he was drafted on to the management team, and my old Northampton team-mate and close friend, John Gregory, remembers him well from his spell at Loftus Road as manager of Queens Park Rangers. John has nothing but the highest praise for the man and I was never less than impressed with his style whenever we got together. Terry was a success even then but he was still keen to learn, and the so-called 'Liverpool Way' and the mystery that was supposed to surround it was something that always intrigued him. He would corner me in the hotel lounge after training and question me about the Anfield set-up, our approach to matches and our training methods. I never felt I had anything to hide, but Terry never believed me – he was convinced that I was keeping something back. Tactics interested him a lot, but at the same time never dominated his approach to the game, and I think that has probably been one of the keys to his success because he has managed to successfully maintain a degree of organisation while at the same time encouraging his players in their freedom of expression.

It has occurred to me on more than one occasion that a managerial partnership comprising Terry Venables and Bob Paisley could have achieved unprecedented success.

9

The England Years – A Tale of Three Managers

It was a Sunday morning in March 1976 and life couldn't have been better. The club was well on its way to the league title, I was planning to take the family out for lunch and looking forward to an afternoon in the garden because even the sun was shining. Then the phone rang.

It was Bob Paisley and the message was short and to the point. 'They want you over in Wales', he said, not giving a moment's thought to the fact that he was breaking some fairly significant news to me. The boss's understatement represented my call-up to Don Revie's England squad and I was surprised, to say the least, because there had been no indication that I figured in his international plans. Like most people in the game, I was aware that Don, who was struggling to find again the formula that had brought him such success at Leeds, had been experimenting with a whole number of different players but my name had never cropped up.

For some bizarre reason my mind flashed back the couple of years to the day I signed for Liverpool and then even further back to that October afternoon when I was summoned to take those vital penalties on the school playing field. It occurred to me that Phil Neal's big opportunities always seemed to happen when least expected. Sue joined me in the hall and we stood looking at each other for a couple of moments – I think she was as taken aback as I was. A couple of minutes earlier our plans had amounted to an afternoon's weeding followed by an evening in front of the television, and now I was facing up to one of the biggest challenges of my career.

Don apparently wanted me in Wales that afternoon and fortunately Wrexham, the team's headquarters, is only about an hour's drive from Merseyside. Looking back I think the fact that the game was being played in the north turned out to be my lucky break because Don clearly had a vast list of potential players, and had the venue been either Cardiff or Swansea he would probably have opted for a replacement full-back in the south. Sue packed me a bag and I called the Anfield caretaker. Half an hour later he let me into the ground to pick up my boots and within three hours of Bob's phone call I was pulling up outside the team's hotel and nervously looking forward to my first meeting with the England Manager.

I soon established that I'd been called up to the squad because Stoke City's Mike Pejic had reported injured the previous evening. The news didn't surprise me because at that time players always seemed to be finding excuses to cry off international duty and naturally I'd heard stories about why. Some said it was because the clubs wanted to give Revie a taste of his own medicine. He'd never been slow to withdraw Leeds United players from mid-week England games to ensure they were fit for vital league matches the following weekend. Now other managers who had released their players in the past and then suffered for their patriotism were delighted to turn the tables on Don whenever they had the chance.

Another source of dissatisfaction was Revie's theory of what life should be like within his England camp. He was a great believer in the idea that the squad should be one big happy family and some of the players couldn't cope with this. In general, the lads felt they were old enough to look after themselves and resented the restrictions the Revie regime imposed upon them ... in fact a number of the lads were really miffed when Don asked them to give a hand with the hoovering or bring in the coal! Unloading my gear from the car, I couldn't help wondering where I fitted in. Naturally I was delighted to figure in the squad whatever the circumstances, but I certainly wasn't any good in the kitchen. Seriously, though, it did occur to me that I might be merely one more club player in form who had happened to catch the manager's eye.

Don met me in the foyer. Most of the lads had yet to arrive but even so he didn't waste a lot of time. From the start he made it plain he was the boss and wanted to be treated as such. My first impression was of an aloof man who demanded that he be treated with respect. Soon the other players began arriving and naturally there was a lot to talk about during the afternoon. It was nice to see old mates again and if any of them were surprised to see me joining their exclusive gathering then they did well to hide it. The match ahead of us was the Welsh FA's centenary international and I remember feeling a certain amount of satisfaction in that my first call-up to the squad was for a fixture with a little bit of prestige attached to it.

That evening I gained my first real insight into life with Don Revie's England and what a joke it turned out to be! No sooner had we finished dinner than Don and his number two, Les Cocker, were ushering us into a private lounge. At first I thought we were going for a chat about the game, but once we were all together out came the bingo cards. It turned out that Don's idea of the perfect evening for his squad was a couple of games of bingo followed by a carpet putting championship. One or two of the more experienced lads were ... shall we say not taking it too seriously, but Don was having none of it. He insisted that everyone had to take part in both games and had even opened a book on the golf.

Now at that time Don was famous for the amount of attention he paid to his team's opponents, although I was yet to receive my first famous dossier, but it was immediately clear that he didn't apply the same depth of research to his own players. For example, he didn't appear to realise that I'd become something of a golfer since moving to Liverpool and when the odds were posted he had me down as an outsider at 10-1. The other Anfield boys couldn't believe it and were arguing in heated whispers about how they could all get a bet on. I could see their anxiety, but even I knew that if Clem, K.K. and Thommo all placed bets on me the boss would twig right away. As the new boy, I didn't want to upset anyone, certainly not as the central figure in a betting coup on my first night with the squad. Eventually they agreed that Ray should have a fiver on me – the stake being put up by the others who would keep quiet in return for a share of the winnings.

Half an hour later I'd cruised through to the semi-finals and a date with Manchester United's Brian Greenhoff. Don was beginning to suspect that he'd been had and the look on his face told the whole story. I was in danger of embarking on the shortest international career on record. It crossed my mind that I could do myself a lot of good by throwing the match, but even in a game of carpet golf such a stunt was unthinkable. I needn't have worried, though, because Brian was a veteran of many of these competitions and seemed to be relishing the cut and thrust of this mindless game. In fact Brian – who is terribly short-sighted – was so desperate to win that he was wearing both his contact lenses and his specs! Naturally I was no match for such single-minded determination and he polished me off with ease. Clem's was the only long face in the house and no one looked more pleased than Don who, minutes before, had been looking odds-on to lose a week's spending money.

I'd joined the squad hoping at best to get a place on the subs' bench, but on the morning of the game the boss took me to one side and told me I'd be playing. It was a big match for Wales and a great stage on which to make my international debut, not that I had any reason to feel lonely because on the night Don fielded a quite unbelievable nine new caps. In addition there were five Liverpool players in the side and my full-back partner from Anfield, Joey Jones, was lining up for the opposition. The game itself turned out to be one of the Revie era's better England performances. I played at right-back but wore number four just to confuse them and we ran out 2-1 winners thanks to goals from Ray Kennedy and Peter Taylor. I was reasonably pleased with my own performance and felt that I had done enough to begin to establish myself at least as a squad member. I'd been particularly delighted with my form in the putting and although I realised I'd been a little on the slow side when it came to the bingo I felt that with a bit more practice and some help from my children I'd soon sharpen up that area of my game as well.

I made the squad again for the end-of-season Home International Championship, but never got off the subs' bench. There were a number of good full-backs around at the time and Revie seemed determined to use all of them – and a few surprises besides. First he tried Dave Clement from Queens Park Rangers and then Mick Mills was given a run before he introduced Colin Todd – a naturally gifted central defender – as a right-back. He went on to try Trevor Cherry and then give a first cap to John Gidman before he somehow remembered me and let me have a second chance. I was beginning to believe all those stories about the Revie selection policy. Perhaps I was just another good First Division player who had happened to play well when the England manager was in the stand. However, I was still being included in the squad so I decided to spend every spare hour perfecting my bingo – which sadly had turned out to be a particular weakness in my game – in the hope of eventually attracting the boss's attention.

I was delighted to get the nod for the tour of the United States, which made a great end to Liverpool's 1976 championship season. I wasn't in the side facing Brazil, but I did start to play five days later when we met Italy in New York. I learned an important lesson in that match when I crossed the path of probably the world's top hatchet man, the notorious Romeo Benetti and showed my inexperience at this level by butting his elbow! Quite honestly it was a blatant cynical foul, a classic of its kind, cleverly executed well out of sight of the referee. The result was a great deal of blood, an early exit for me and my first look at the inside of a casuality wing of a New York hospital. We were 1-0 down when I went off but by the time I got back to the stadium the boys had turned the match, much to the anger of the huge Italian contingent in the crowd. In the end we ran out 3-2 winners thanks to a couple of goals from Mick Channon and a third from Phil Thompson – the only goal of his international career. It was England's sole win of the tour and I was sorry that I could not claim to have played a more significant part in it.

Back in England Don Revie seemed to see me as nothing more than a squad member and it turned out to be a year almost to the day before I next played for England. The intervening period was quite an eventful one: Liverpool went from strength to strength while the national side came in for increasing criticism from the press and developed a kind of Wembley phobia, losing to both Holland and Wales and putting up indifferent performances against the Republic of Ireland and Finland.

As a member of the squad I was getting plenty of opportunity to assess the Revie style of management even though I was doing precious little to broaden my experience as an international player. The man was never a popular figure with the public, who resented the fact that his success at Leeds had been born out of such a negative style of play. They had tolerated his appointment as the England manager because after the World Cup disappointment of 1970 and Sir Alf Ramsey's failure to put together a side capable of qualifying in 1974, everyone was desperate for success on the field. It was generally accepted that it was better for England to become unpopular winners than to continue as gracious losers.

When Revie failed to deliver the goods quickly enough the fans and the media were soon on his back. He chopped and changed the side at whim and never allowed any team that he selected to settle down and establish a set pattern of play. This was the policy that puzzled me most because at Leeds, continuity was the element he cherished the most. Worse still, he failed to realise that the family atmosphere he had created so successfully at Leeds couldn't work at international level. I found the bingo and carpet golf an amusing eccentricity the first time I was called up for the squad, but after a while they began to get on my nerves. I could see two fat ladies in my sleep and whenever the kids at home mentioned two little ducks I automatically shouted 'quack quack'!

Seriously, I felt we were being treated like children rather than the experienced and conscientious professionals we were and I know many of the other lads agreed with me. Gerry Francis, who was then the England captain, was forever trying to get out of taking part in the silly games but the boss would have none of it. In the end Gerry would make a big show of placing his bet at the beginning of the competition and then make sure he was eliminated in the first round. He'd turn around and carefully comb his hair in front of the mirror and then sneak off to his room – checking his hair once more – as soon as the competition was safely underway. I suppose you're entitled to get away with that when you're the England captain, but a new boy like me was left with no alternative but to grin and bear it.

I won seven caps in all during Revie's reign and I will naturally always be grateful that he gave me my first chance, but by the time we went on the South American tour of 1977, it was clear that something had to give. I'd just about established myself in the number two shirt at that stage but morale within the squad was pretty low. Rumours were beginning to circulate about Don's future and when he announced he would be joining the squad in

South America rather than travelling with it, some of us began to wonder whether he was facing the sack. As it turned out, the manager beat the FA to it, and lined himself up with a big-money job in the Middle East. News of his resignation was broken by the *Daily Mail* journalist Jeff Powell. He collected himself a world exclusive and Don pocketed even more spending money.

Rumours about Revie's future had been rife when we left England and cast a huge shadow over the whole tour. Under the circumstances our record of three draws from the three games played doesn't look too bad, particularly when you take into account the fact that Brazil, Argentina and Uruguay formed the opposition, and we were expected to get the right results in a far from ideal environment. I remember feeling sorry for Les Cocker, who had been a loyal aide to Revie for so many years only to be left high and dry when the going got tough. He was our sole inspiration in South America and I think all the lads appreciated that he was putting on a brave face for the sake of team spirit.

Describing Les as being left 'high and dry' reminds me of one of the few funny stories from what turned out to be a pretty miserable experience. One afternoon, most of the lads were lounging around the pool trying to cope with the extremes of the South American heat. Spirits weren't particularly high and a couple of the squad's more experienced jokers, Mick Channon and Kevin Keegan, thought it was time to liven things up. Little Les was flat out on a sun-lounger recovering from a hard morning barking out orders on the training field and, urged on by the rest of us, Micky and K.K. decided to get their own back. They crept up behind the unsuspecting trainer and tipped him headlong into the swimming-pool, much to the delight of everyone watching.

Seconds later Les was thrashing around like a madman and screaming for help. At first everyone thought he in turn was trying to get his own back and the more he struggled the more everyone cheered and laughed. A full half minute went by before someone realised that Les couldn't swim and by the time Dave Watson had dived in and dragged him to the side in true lifeguard tradition our two favourite jokers had beaten a hasty retreat. Les was damp but not defeated, though, because the next day on the training pitch he had the last laugh when he put us through his most gruelling, leg-wobbling, stomach-churning training session. Funnily enough there wasn't a single voice raised in dissent and I've never seen Mick Channon train so hard in his life.

Reflecting on the Revie era it seems to me that Don enjoyed 'dishing it out' but couldn't take the pressure when the tide turned. Many of us felt he should have had the courage to admit that the job wasn't working out instead of using his reputation as England manager to negotiate a lucrative overseas contract and then leaving everyone high and dry without a second thought. In the beginning the Revie era promised so much, but in the end it turned out to be one of our national game's most unsatisfactory episodes.

The man charged with the responsibility of restoring dignity to the England job was Ron Greenwood. His was an appointment that surprised many people but in my view, on reflection, it turned out to be the best possible move. After Revie, there was the need for stability and, more importantly, for intergrity – Ron brought both qualities to the job and remains perhaps the greatest single influence on my career. I have only the highest praise for him not just as a manager, but, more importantly, as a man.

From the word go Ron treated his England players like adults and Revie's contrived family atmosphere went right out of the window. Don't get me wrong, he was still keen to establish a good spirit within the squad, but he allowed that spirit to develop naturally, and, as with most things in life, if you allow something to develop in its own time it will prove stronger and more beneficial in the long run. This was the Ron Greenwood way. As with Revie, we would all meet at a North London hotel on the Sunday before a mid-week game. Ron would welcome each of us individually with perhaps a word or two about the previous day's games and a check-up for injuries, and then we'd all get together for dinner and a general natter about the match. The chat would take place in a relaxed atmosphere and there were certainly no dossiers. Afterwards Ron would encourage us to go down to the local pub for a couple of beers. 'Off you go and pick the team', he would say with a wry smile.

He knew that even though we were the people directly concerned, we were no different from any other group of blokes together in a pub. We all knew which line-up we would choose and, just like anyone else, we all thought we knew far more than the England manager. I can almost hear you muttering about slack attitude but you would be wrong. For a start there's no harm in a couple of beers on a Sunday, but more importantly Ron was demonstrating his trust in us. In all the years I was a part of the England set-up under Ron, I never saw a single player take advantage of his attitude. He commanded respect amongst everyone.

Ron inherited the England team at a time when 'Wembley phobia' was at its worst. It didn't seem to matter how weak the opposition was, the lads just didn't seem to be able to settle and get the right results there, so when he set about picking his first team, Ron was clearly conscious of the need to establish some stability. The sight of the once proud white shirts of England trooping off the Wembley turf hanging limply from the drooping shoulders of embarrassed players to the accompaniment of boos and chants of 'what a load of rubbish' would have to be swept aside quickly with an enthusiastic, spirited display to show the Wembley crowd that a new, bright era in English football had begun.

Ron surprised everyone, including me, by selecting a line-up that included no fewer than seven Liverpool players and earned a final unexpected cap for Ian Callaghan at the ripe old age of 35. Naturally I was thrilled to be one of Ron's 'magnificent seven' and the prospect of playing in the national team surrounded by the same players that I trained and played with every day of the week appealed to me enormously, but I had to admit that it was an extremely bold and adventurous step for a new manager. It was a move that had brought success to many of the Eastern European nations but, to my certain knowledge, had never before been tried in the West.

The advantages of Ron's scheme were obvious. After Revie, it was a relief just to know a few of the players' names, but it wasn't, as they say all right on the night and the Anfield influence didn't prove powerful enough to overcome the Wembley jinx. The part-timers from Switzerland held us to an embarrassing 0-0 draw and it was a display that earned us every insult in the book. The almost obligatory slow handclap from the fans was even louder and lasted even longer than usual, continuing well after most of us had drowned our sorrows in the bath and the bar. Public humiliation on the back pages of the national newspapers the next day was no more than any of us expected and when the 'magnificent seven' returned to Anfield the next day, the remaining four members of the first team wasted no time in reminding us that our performance the previous night merely emphasised their importance in the success of Liverpool Football Club.

Since my days at Northampton I'd learned to take little notice of the newspapers. Dave Bowen used to refer to them as tomorrow's fish and chip wrappings, but that morning it was impossible to ignore them. It was a savage mauling, worse than anything I'd seen since the humiliating Wembley draw with Poland that kept us out of the 1974 World Cup finals. It was probably no more than the players deserved, but I do think that the manager was owed a little more consideration, particularly as it was only his first game in charge. However, depressing though things were, I already had a feeling that Ron Greenwood would get things right and that under his leadership England's future would be bright. I was just hoping that I would remain a part of his plans. Ron didn't let his disappointment show publicly and he began his rebuilding task in earnest. He travelled the length and breadth of the country watching potential players but unlike his predecessor he wasn't a man to chop and change his line-up at the whim of the press.

His right-hand man was the late Bill Taylor, a quiet, perhaps dour man who was nevertheless an excellent coach, and Ron drafted World Cup hero Geoff Hurst into his back-room team to help with the training. Ron would always be out on the field when we trained and he was forever looking for innovative routines to keep the sessions interesting and enjoyable. In Geoff Hurst of course he had the ideal man to put his ideas into practice because he was still young enough and fit enough to demonstrate the techniques. Ron is a great observer and would often store up something he had noted about your game for weeks until he next saw you. Then there'd be a quiet word, a point made and advice accepted. It was a great way to work and even at that stage of my career I felt I was still learning useful things.

Ron's concern for his players wasn't confined to the international stage. I remember him making a point of speaking to me at Anfield an hour or so before an important European Cup tie against a Polish side. He'd been watching Poland a few weeks before and had picked up a couple of details about the winger's play. He marked my card and sure enough he was absolutely right. I played well that night and felt I owed at least a part of that to Ron Greenwood. I gained the majority of my England caps under Greenwood and thoroughly enjoyed the experience, but there were two incidents towards the end of his reign which must be mentioned.

The first came on the way back from Budapest in June

1981. We had won the game against Hungary but had nevertheless been all but mathematically eliminated from the 1982 World Cup finals in Spain thanks to our defeat against Switzerland in Basle a few days earlier. All our heads were down and no one was looking forward to the news conference at Heathrow. Ron had spent most of the journey deep in conversation with Bill Taylor and Geoff Hurst, but about 15 minutes before we landed he called the lads together. There was a curtain behind our section of the plane and someone drew it across to give us some privacy. Ron told us how upset he had been by the defeat and how he felt he had let the country down, then stunned each and every one of us by announcing that he proposed to use the news conference to announce his resignation.

There was silence for a moment and then loud protests, particularly from the senior players in the squad. Clem was one of the first to chip in. 'If you quit then we may as well all throw our boots away'! Ron looked genuinely puzzled by the depth of feeling, but was obviously influenced by the bond of comradeship which united us all. It was a bond which Ron himself had created and it was unthinkable from our point of view that he should consider himself personally responsible for our failure against the Danes.

We all believed that England had begun to achieve things under Ron Greenwood and that the squad's future should remain in his hands. The arguments that he should stay were among the most passionate I had heard from a group of footballers but nevertheless it was touch and go for several minutes. At one stage it looked a distinct possibility that the waiting press would be treated not only to the surprise resignation of the England manager but also the mass resignation of the England squad.

In the nick of time, though, good sense prevailed and Ron agreed to reconsider his position. In another man his behaviour on that plane might have been considered a classic case of over-reaction or worse still a cheap stunt aimed at canvassing as much support as possible before what was certain to be an awkward news conference. In Ron's case, though, there was no question that it was a step taken with genuine feeling and only after considerable thought. He didn't try to blame the players for what had happened in Oslo, or for that matter on the other occasions when we should have made sure of qualifying. The responsibility was his and his alone, or so he thought, and as a man with such high principles he felt he had let the nation down and should do the honourable thing and resign, leaving the way clear for another man. Fortunately, though, this was one of the few occasions in my experience when player power succeeded and Ron went on to lead the squad in Spain.

The second incident came in the weeks leading up to the World Cup finals. England, now qualified – thanks to two Trevor Brooking goals in the Nep Stadium in Hungary – had got themselves double-booked with games against Iceland and Finland on successive days. The main body of the squad went to Helsinki to 'Finnish' them off while the rest were sent to Reykjavik for the other match. Ron was due to announce his squad for Spain at the end of that week but already he had made it clear that the lads in Finland had booked their tickets. That left just six places to fill and these would be going to players from the squad in Iceland.

I was one of those players fighting for my place in Reykjavik and you can't imagine how tense things were. Most of us were frightened of our own shadows, fearing that either we would be injured or make the sort of mistake that would earn us the thumbs-down. Needless to say we didn't play well there, scraping a 1-1 draw, and the next day the tension was compounded when the other lads romped home 4-1. Back in England I must have been hell to live with as I waited for that call. I had been a senior member of the England squad for some considerable time but I was analysing my form and agonising over the future 24 hours a day. At 31, and with a number of good young players on the verge of the national side, I knew that realistically this would be my one and only chance to play in the World Cup finals.

With the domestic season over, I didn't even have my Liverpool team-mates to help take my mind off things and wandering around at home trying to find things to do I just irritated Sue, who wasn't used to having me under her feet all the time. Each time the phone rang it nearly scared me out of my skin and I cannot remember a week either before or since when I've answered so many irrelevant calls. Finally, though, at the end of what was surely the longest week of my life, the call I'd been waiting for came through from Lancaster Gate and I'd made it into the final squad for England's first appearance in the finals for 12 years.

Spain was a great experience although our failure to qualify for the quarter-finals was a grave disappointment. I wasn't named in the starting line-up for the first game against France, but made it to the subs' bench. I came on for just 17 seconds in place of an injured Kenny Sansom and although I didn't get a kick I did manage to take a throw-in. Ron was clearly impressed because I was promoted to the team for the next match against Kuwait. The record book shows that we failed to progress beyond the opening round of the competition even though we didn't lose a game. To be eliminated in this way was a bitter pill to swallow because, although deep down I think we all knew that we weren't good enough to take the title, we did want to send the retiring Ron Greenwood out on a high.

Like everyone else I can only sit back and wonder what would have happened had our two most influential players, Kevin Keegan and Trevor Brooking, not been struck down with mysterious but serious back and pelvic injuries. In our last crucial group game, in which we needed to beat the host nation Spain, Ron took his last England gamble and pushed them both into the action as our ambitions for a place in the quarter-finals were rapidly sliding away. I was on the bench that night as they both went on as substitutes and we all knew they were nowhere near fit enough for a match as important as that one. Nevertheless there wasn't a voice raised in criticism because both Kevin and Trevor were world-class players and if ever there was a moment in English football history when a gamble was justified this was it. The cruel irony was that the move half-worked because towards the end of the game we created two great chances, one falling to Trevor and the other to Kevin. We watched helplessly from the sidelines as both went begging, knowing full well that both would have been comfortably tucked away had the players been fit.

The final whistle signalled our World Cup exit and the curtain was drawn on Ron Greenwood's reign as England's manager. He has had his critics, I know, and many point to his failure to win a European championship, but I have only fond memories of the man. He took over a thankless job at a particularly difficult time for the English game and he restored the dignity and pride of the national side. Most of all he created an environment in which players wanted to win caps again. Ron Greenwood remains one of the few men I would happily turn to for advice on my own managerial problems. He will always find the time to talk and his opinions are always worth listening to.

Greenwood gave way to Bobby Robson – the third England manager I played under – and his attitude to the game was different from anything I'd experienced before. His whole approach was based on fear. Not, as you might expect, on fear of him, but instead on a fear of the opposition! A typical Robson team-talk would go on for hours – no wonder the Ipswich lads in the squad had nicknamed him 'Mogadon'. I remember before one game he called the squad together 'for ten minutes' just before we were due to go into dinner. Three hours later, with most of us starving, the head waiter knocked on the door, threw the boss the keys and asked us to lock up the restaurant when we'd finished.

Mind you, that was the last time we had trouble with a head waiter because soon after Robson took over he decided we should swap the luxury of hotel life for the spartan existence at Bisham Abbey. The actual sporting facilities there are first-rate but our dormitories made Butlins at Pwellhi seem like The Dorchester! There were two beds and no room for anything else – thank goodness I was sharing with little Sammy Lee. The food, good wholesome English fare, was served up in a communal dining-room where we all sat around a giant table. The only concession made to the fact that we were supposed to be the cream of the nation's footballers was that unlike the other residents we didn't have to clear our own pots away and do the washing-up.

Naturally, most of the lads were soon moaning but it took the sight of Trevor Francis queueing for an hour to use the building's one payphone with his jacket pockets weighted down to his ankles with 10ps so that he could ring his wife in Italy to provoke the formal protest. Eventually a small deputation of senior players met with the manager and pointed out to him in the most diplomatic way possible that we would all feel more relaxed in a proper hotel. Not necessarily the five-star life of luxury, but something a little more up-market all the same. I think he accepted our position because Bisham Abbey hasn't been mentioned since.

In the run-up to any international fixture Robson would spend hours telling us how good the opposition was without ever giving us any real advice on how to play against them. Before his first game in charge – against Denmark – he had us living in fear of the 'Great Danes' for four days before the match. He showed us videos of them in action and at one stage I was convinced he was going to bring out the old Kirk Douglas film *The Vikings* to emphasise his point. We drew 2-all, which was a good result under the circumstances, but the manager had got some of the lads so wound up that I'm surprised they managed even a wink of sleep the night before the game.

Irritating too was Robson's relationship with the press. He took a totally different tack from Ron Greenwood and seemed obsessed with the notion that he had to keep the reporters on his side at any price. Most of them seemed to enjoy open access to him and I for one felt that this sort of contact rendered him particularly vulnerable to manipulation. At one stage it was clear to me and a number of other people involved in the game that the press was enjoying unprecedented influence when it came to picking the England team. For example, certain players on the fringes of the national squad would begin attracting rave notices in the newspapers a couple of weeks before an international. Then one or two of the top columnists would begin tipping a particular lad for an international cap and quoting inside sources. Sure enough, when the squad was announced that particular player would be in it.

I played 11 times for England after Bobby Robson took over as manager and eventually stepped down from the international stage in 1983 with 50 caps – a record for an England full-back. Towards the end of my international career, though, I had begun to feel uneasy about the way England squads were being selected. Too many different players were winning odd caps and the continuity that had been so important under Greenwood seemed to be disappearing. Fans of the England manager will argue that he needed to experiment to find the right balance for Mexico – I felt there was a very real danger that we would turn full circle and go back to the dark days under Revie when the manager's indecision was final.

10

The Fans and the Press – My Loves and Hates

Two groups more than any others are responsible for perpetuating football as our national game and I've seen the best and worst of each of them. The same reporters I've nattered with at evening functions have abused me from the terraces the following Saturday afternoon and reporters I've shared a post-match drink with have torn me to shreds in their columns the next day.

When you get down to basics, football is an arm of the entertainment business and when people are paying for the privilege of watching you play they are entitled to criticise your performance. Criticism is the right of every fan and the same must apply to journalists but, on the other hand, they are paid well for what they write and I would expect their opinions to be based on a greater understanding of the game. Unfortunately, too often their so-called analysis is as 'knee-jerk' a judgement as that of the average supporter.

Mike Langley – the *Sunday People*'s self-styled 'voice of sport' – is a classic of the type. I remember once, after a game at Highbury, climbing on to the Liverpool team coach to hear Mike describing me and Terry McDermott as 'just a couple of ordinary England players' for the benefit of thousands of listeners to the BBC's Sports Report. Normally I don't let criticism worry me too much but for some reason on this occasion I was incensed. Who was he to talk? What standard had he ever reached in the game and anyway what exactly was an 'ordinary England player'?

Playing for England meant a great deal to me. I realise that quite a few players managed the odd cap during the reign of Revie and to a certain extent during the early Greenwood period, but to have made a string of international appearances and to have become established in the national side was something I considered to be one of the main achievements of my career. For Mike to dismiss the achievement so glibly was an insult. I don't believe there is any such thing as an ordinary England player. To gain even one England cap is a clear indication that you have been recognised as one of the top dozen footballers in the nation at that particular time. I won more England caps than any other full-back yet whenever a squad was about to be announced I still felt the old butterflies in the stomach as I waited to see whether or not I would be included.

If Mike had ever played the game at any sort of level I'm sure he would have understood a little bit about the sort of pride a player feels when he represents England and the sense of achievement it gives him. To dismiss it the way he did is not only glib, it's downright unfair. And before you start thinking that I'm being over-sensitive, even a lad as easy-going as Terry Mac was as hurt as I was once I'd managed to get him to understand exactly what Mike had meant. Maybe it seems a trivial complaint to level against a journalist like Mike who, like Domestos, has been a household name for decades, but it sticks in my mind more than many of the other criticisms that have been levelled at me over the years. Consider it this way: Mike has climbed to the top of the journalistic tree and I'd never dream of describing him here as 'just another ordinary reporter'.

Mike Langley, though, was merely a part of a sort of Fleet Street mafia that dogged the northern players during Ron Greenwood's reign as England manager. The rivalry

'Come on Mick, you'll have to do better than that!' – a warning to my full-back rival as we prepare for Spain. Bob Thomas

ABOVE: *Spot the new recruit – Northampton Town, 1967.* Northampton Chronicle & Echo

RIGHT: *Off to Workington on an overnight trip – at Northampton these sort of scenes warranted a photograph!* Bob Thomas

ABOVE: *Bill Dodgin Jnr takes over at the County Ground and things begin to look up.* Bob Thomas

LEFT: *Emergency keeper in my final game. Little did I know that my dream move to Anfield was just two days away.* Bob Thomas

My first League Championship and Emlyn leads the celebrations – needless to say someone else bought the Champagne. Bob Thomas

TOP: *Goal! Nothing beats that feeling.* Harry Ormesher

BOTTOM: *'Now behave yourself, Terry, or you can't come out with us tonight!'*

TOP: *Romeo Benetti of Italy, gentle by name, anything but by nature.* Colorsport

BOTTOM: *You can never find a referee when you really need one!* Bob Thomas

TOP: *My back-room staff – wife Sue and children Ashley and Natasha.* Daily Mirror

BOTTOM: *My testimonial game against Everton – the one night I was able to forget my worries.* Bob Thomas

Bolton – the start of a new phase in my career. Bob Thomas

between the north and south is legendary and the London-based writers have always seemed to resent the success of the northern clubs. I spent my entire England career reading stories in the national newspapers that made it plain I wasn't up to the job. The problem stemmed from the fact that there were a number of promising full-backs based at London clubs and the press wanted me out of the side. Often the fans appeared to be in much the same frame of mind mainly, I suppose, because the hard core of England's mid-week Wembley support is south-east based. I had a pretty hard time as a result and I particularly remember one game mid-way through my England years in which Ray Clemence and I were booed for apparent time-wasting. I had passed the ball back to him – following instructions from the manager not to take chances on an especially difficult surface – but the fans were having none of it. They hissed and whistled and generally voiced their displeasure, yet minutes later when Trevor Brooking did exactly the same thing there was resounding applause for his safety-first tactics.

I believe that the Football Association is making a grave mistake by insisting that England play all their home matches at Wembley. It is a fine stadium without doubt, and a daunting international venue, but when there are only a few thousand people watching, the event is stripped of its atmosphere. Why not take the international roadshow north to Manchester, Liverpool or Newcastle and give the fans there a chance to roar at the national team? Then the opposition would see just how partisan an English crowd can be. If the Football Association were prepared to charge a realistic price for tickets and not demand the inflated amounts they insist upon at Wembley then the stadium would be full and the crowd would be right behind the players. I reckon this would be a sure-fire way to overcome that so-called Wembley jinx. However, while Wembley remains the chosen venue, I'm afraid that only players based with Southern clubs can expect to have the fans on their side.

When I was fortunate enough to complete my ten years at Anfield with a testimonial season, the fans were brilliant. They more than repaid me for a decade's blood, sweat and tears with their response to the many functions that were staged. The organisers of the testimonial drew up a punishing schedule and some weeks I found myself out and about at pubs and clubs five nights running. Fitting in this sort of routine around training would ordinarily have proved very difficult, but no matter where I went the reception was tremendous and I loved every minute of it.

My success as a footballer has helped provide me and my family with the good things in life and for that I shall be eternally grateful, but it is easy to take success and the rewards it brings for granted. Some of the people I met during my testimonial year served as a timely reminder of the sacrifices many fans have to make to follow the game. Everyone knows just how serious the problem of unemployment is on Merseyside, yet many of the people who line up in the dole queues on a Monday have spent their last couple of pounds at the Anfield turnstiles the previous Saturday – such is their dedication to the club and passion for the game.

I'm sure this 24-hour-a-day commitment to football has a great deal to do with the success of both Liverpool clubs. On Merseyside you are not allowed to forget the game or its importance to the community for a moment. The Kop at Anfield is famous the world over and visiting teams are almost always in awe of it. Everyone can picture in their mind's eye the image of The Kop in full voice singing 'You'll Never Walk Alone' and remembers how the fans have a special spot in their hearts for goalkeepers, but few realise just how great their influence is over the Liverpool players.

Naturally, I can speak only for myself but I remember very well at least two occasions when The Kop helped me. The first came during a period when my form seemed to have mysteriously left me. I couldn't pinpoint just why I was playing badly but the spark had certainly fizzled out temporarily. Somehow, though, I'd kept my place in the side and Manchester City were the visitors. Mid-way through the game and with the scores level, we were awarded a penalty at the Kop end of the ground. I was the recognised penalty-taker in the side but I had my doubts that afternoon. To be frank, I was looking to decline until the fans began to roar my name making it clear that they expected me to take the kick. My confidence soared and I stepped up to the ball with a new spring in my stride and gave big Joe Corrigan no chance. The Kop had psyched me up to take the kick and the goal was for them.

A couple of seasons later they once again proved an inspiration to my game. It was 1982-83, immediately following the World Cup and Spain, and the spectacle of the Brazilian genius, were still fresh in everyone's minds. As a full-back, I love going forward and I believe one of the great strengths of my game has been my ability to lend support in attack. I'm sure the origins of this are founded in my experience at Northampton, where I spent a lot of my time as a midfield player, but nevertheless I have never been afraid of taking a shot when the opportunity arises and have scored my fair share of goals over the years. I wasn't conscious of approaching the game any differently at the time, all I did know was that the goals seemed to be coming with ease and not just from the penalty spot. The phenomenon hadn't escaped the fans, however, and whenever I collected a ball within range of goal they began chanting 'Zico' 'Zico!', willing me to have a go. I could sense my right foot almost twitching as I homed in on the goal and the roar of the crowd encouraged me to have a go when otherwise perhaps I might have passed. The result was a string of goals that might never have happened!

In my early years as a player at Northampton, the attentions of the local press were flattering. The club was on the slide and had very little going for it but each year as a new season loomed the local scribes would be out predicting that the 'Cobblers' had a new attitude and were determined to 'turn the tide'. I was one of the club's few prospects and I came in for my fair share of attention. Almost always the words were favourable and I studiously stuck the clippings into my scrapbook for posterity.

My transfer to Liverpool catapulted me not only into a different class of football but also into a different league of journalism. Suddenly I was being exposed on a national stage and once I made the breakthrough into the England side I soon realised that I had become fair game for any reporter. To say I wasn't a popular player with the press would be verging on the understatement. The sports writers quickly picked up on my shortcomings as a tackler – the so-called weakness in my game – and although I went on to win a record number of caps, they never really accepted me as an established England player. You learn to accept criticism in this game and on many occasions you can either scoff at it or ignore it. Only rarely is the attack justified and sufficient to make you reassess your position. I do remember one such occasion and it involved John Sadler from The *Sun*.

Now John isn't a particularly popular writer with many of the players and I remember very well the reaction of many of the England lads when news broke that he was to succeed Frank Clough as the newspaper's main football writer. Frank was a highly-respected figure and could be relied upon to present a balanced picture on almost any issue. John, on the other hand, was very self-opinionated and belonged to the school of thought that believed the facts should be made to fit the story. However, there was one occasion when he did me the greatest of favours. Liverpool had been playing in London and needless to say the press were on our backs. The sort of resentment some of the journalists felt about the Anfield success story was quite unbelievable. Anyway, after this particular game John remarked that I had performed as if I was playing in a

Savile Row suit. I was incensed at the time, but gradually I started to think about what he was implying and, in the end, reluctantly, I was forced to admit that he had a point. I hadn't shirked, that would never be my way, but maybe I hadn't mixed it quite as much as I should have done. Sure, I prided myself on being a polished player but maybe I needed to get stuck in a little bit more. John's words were well and truly hammered home and I resolved to adjust my approach as a result.

That's the end of my 'be nice to John Sadler' passage because Sue would never agree with me. To her, John is the journalist she would most like to strangle and over the years she has collected her own 'black library' of some of the nastier things he has written about me. I'm afraid she takes the criticism to heart a lot more than I do. She feels some of the attacks are too personal and don't reflect the feelings of the majority of fans. What is more, she sees a lot more of the people outside the game who buy the newspapers and take the stories as gospel. Sue's had to comfort Ashley and Natasha when the other kids have had a go at them in the playground and she has been forced to put up with the moaners who think I'm public property 24 hours a day, so I suppose she's got a right to get annoyed.

Privacy is something the fans tend to overlook and sometimes it can get quite tiresome. I've always done my best to accommodate the supporters, signing countless autographs and appearing at functions, but you have to draw the line somewhere and nothing annoys me more than to be interrupted when I'm enjoying a quiet meal out with the family. How would you feel if your were half-way through your steak and salad and catching up on the week's news when some complete stranger walks up to you and thrusts a paper napkin under your nose, demanding: 'Sign this!'?

This is not an exaggeration, it has happened to me on many occasions. Sometimes, more out of shock than anything else, I have signed my name and the autograph-hunter has disappeared without so much as a 'thank you'. On other occasions I have looked up and asked the person to wait until I have finished my meal. A reasonable enough request, but a response that usually generates abuse. Sue says I'm too easy-going.

Then there are the 'smart Alecs' who see you in an hotel and think you're there to be made fun of. Perhaps they score points with their mates, I don't know, but as far as I'm concerned they're boring. Their favourite jibe goes something like this: 'Hey, Nealy! You're rubbish!'. I hate to disappoint them but it never bothers me. I just look at the beer-belly bulging over the belt and pity them for what they've missed. Imagine having to face your mates in the bar the day you've been dropped from the Sunday pub team!

The Merseyside press boys have been good to me generally, but even though they're dealing with the club week-in week-out they don't make any concessions. They produced a really despicable story about Mark Lawrenson, which suggested he was gay, and no matter how often he denied it some of the mud stuck. To this day nobody knows where the tale originated but it succeeded in causing a lot of anguish at the time. Then there was the time a couple of days before Liverpool were due to fly out to Athens to face the Greek champions. It was six in the morning when the phone woke me and my first thought was that something had happened to one of my family. I grabbed the receiver expecting to hear a familiar voice but instead, behind the hiss of the long-distance line, was a Greek jabbering at me in broken English. He wanted some exclusive team news and what made matters worse was the fact that one of the local reporters, Ian Hargreaves, had given him my home number. What a liberty!

During the 1985-86 season I spent time in the press box and watched the football specialists at work for the first time. Maybe this is my chance to get a little bit of my own back, but I have to say I was far from impressed. When a goal was scored the move leading up to it was written up by consensus. 'Who crossed it?' 'Did Sammy Lee get a touch?' 'What was the free kick for?' No one seemed to have the first clue about what was happening. If players approached their jobs in such a slapdash fashion they'd be crucified in the newspapers.

Then there's the business of angles. The factual no-nonsense match report appears to be a thing of the past – today the specialists tend to base their stories around individuals and bend the facts to suit the message they want to get across. Liverpool's Paul Walsh is one of the most talented players in the game. I've spoken out in his favour more than most but I have to admit that he's enjoyed more than his share of media hype. Reporters seem to have arrived at Anfield to write a story about Paul rather than to report on the game and the same has been true of a couple of other players. This puts them under an intolerable amount of pressure and tends to build them up into something they are not. Then, when they slip up, the criticism is venomous and the confidence of a young, impressionable player can be shattered in the space of a few lines.

When I moved into football management I had to decide at once how I was going to handle press relations and I'm afraid my approach wasn't the most popular. Charlie Wright had been soft and the local journalists had taken liberties. They were eroding confidence in the club and taking advantage of their access to certain players by writing articles that unfairly undermined Bolton Wanderers. My first move was to ban reporters from the team coach. Journeys home from away games had been ideal for picking up the sort of gossip that formed the basis of the knocking stories and I didn't want it to continue. I felt the players were entitled to their privacy and should be allowed to unwind after matches without worrying about whether or not their comments would appear in the press. It was an unpopular move and I'm sure I've come in for a great deal of criticism as a result, but I'm convinced I acted in the best interests of the club.

The fans and the press are vital to the game and as footballers we must never forget that our sport is a part of the entertainment business. However, there is a thin dividing line between the public side of our lives and our right to privacy, and it is this division that I am anxious to preserve.

11

My Back-Room Staff

Stability has been the cornerstone of my success as a footballer and I have one person to thank for it – my wife Sue. We met as class-mates at the age of 14 and began going out about a year later. We were engaged when we were 19 and everyone said we were mad when we tied the knot at 20, but we're still going strong. If it wasn't for me and our son Ashley then I'm sure she would take no interest in the game, but as it is she turns up week-in week-out and has shared in all the ups and downs of my professional career. We've climbed a steep hill together and sometimes when we look back to the early years we have to admit that it is a miracle that our relationship has survived.

At Northampton, money was so tight that even now I still have to marvel at the way Sue managed the household accounts. Often we would get by only because of the generosity of our families who would bail us out with a basket of groceries when we didn't know where the next meal was coming from. Some weeks the club couldn't pay us on a Friday and we were kept waiting until the following week, and Saturday's takings had been safely banked before our wage packets arrived, such was the never-ending struggle for survival in the fourth division of the Football League.

Sue grumbled only once and that taught me a lesson I remembered for the rest of my playing career. Northampton had been playing Hereford and Phil Neal had got himself involved in something of a running feud with

Dudley Tyler. Late in the second half the inevitable happened and I was sent off for the first and only time in my career. Naturally the club wasted no time in fining me a week's wages – in view of their financial predicament it was too good an opportunity to miss – and I went home that evening to break the news to Sue. I'd prepared a speech of explanation that contained words like 'victimised' and 'provocation' but she would have none of it. She cut me dead with the realities of life on the bread-line and I resolved there and then to get on with the game and not to join the growing ranks of the so-called 'bad men' of soccer.

Although I'd been involved in football since way before we began dating, it never occurred to me to take Sue to a game. The only exception came one Christmas when I took her to Northampton's home match on Boxing Day, otherwise the only contact she had with the game was in a Wellingborough pub where she used to meet me after training. Even so, when things were tough and I was seriously considering calling it a day, it was Sue who persuaded me to put off the final decision, convinced that better times lay just around the corner. Signing for Liverpool was our turning point.

In a decade at Liverpool I enjoyed tremendous success and our lifestyle was revolutionised. After wondering where the next meal might be coming from we suddenly found ourselves with money in the bank and a nice home in a smart part of town. Never for a moment, though, did we lose sight of what we had emerged from and this has ensured that our feet have remained firmly on the ground. I've always been conscious of the uncertainty that surrounds soccer as a career and have made plans to cope with any eventuality. I haven't been tempted to put money into risky business ventures, although I've lost count of the number of offers that I've had. The latest came within days of starting work at Bolton and was bizarre even by football standards.

A guy I'd never met before rang the club and asked for an appointment with me to discuss a business venture. He arrived laden down with architect's plans for a swish new squash club somewhere between Manchester and Liverpool. He was full of big ideas and his patter was good but it soon became clear that he was expecting me to produce my cheque book and get involved. I had no intention of going into business with someone I'd never met but he'd reached the punchline before I'd even got a word in. 'So how about it, Phil? Fifty grand for starters and we'll split any of the unexpected extras down the middle'! I burst out laughing and the other chap shot me an accusing glance. 'What's the problem?' he asked.

I could have thought of a hundred but instead I replied. 'Well, for starters I never do business with someone I don't know and secondly I couldn't lay my hands on fifty thousand pounds even if I wanted to'. 'But you've just had your testimonial, you must have the money', he insisted. Eventually I got the message across that I wasn't interested but even then he wasn't going to give up without a fight. 'OK Phil, if you don't want to come in then what about some of the other lads at Liverpool? Surely one of them has got a bit of spare cash he wants to put to good use.' 'Phone the club', I replied, showing him the door, knowing full well that he'd be joining a far longer queue at Anfield than he'd faced at Burnden Park.

And I promise you this wasn't an isolated incident. Every wide boy with an eye to the main chance and an easy buck thinks footballers have more money than sense and are a soft touch. Unfortunately in many cases they are right, and once they get their teeth into a lad it's surprising just how quickly and effectively they can bleed him dry. At Liverpool a couple of the lads were well and truly taken by a man they trusted enough to appoint as their agent. In the end he repaid their confidence by disappearing with a great deal of their money, cash that could have been wisely invested as a nest egg for the end of their playing days.

A big club like Liverpool attracts its fair share of smooth-talking hangers-on, and if you want a first-hand look at most of northern soccer's parasites under one roof then get yourself an invitation either to the players' lounge or the sponsors' bar when 'The Reds' meet Manchester United. You can't move for leather coats and furs and the chat washes over you like a barrel of sun-tan oil. The men are rich and mostly in their forties or fifties, their women are glamorous if a little past their best. They call you 'Phil' or 'Kenny' and greet you like a brother or a long-lost mate. All the time, though, they're doing the mental arithmetic: How much is this boy worth? Will he come in with me? Is he important enough? Sadly, too many of the players I've worked alongside have been taken in by the glib chat and then have been parted from their money. Fortunately, Sue counts highly among her characteristics the ability to spot insincerity and I have to admit that there have been a number of occasions when she has picked up on the bad vibes way before I have. I'm cautious but in the end trusting by nature, and I'm sure Sue has saved me from my fair share of financial scrapes.

As it is, I've invested wisely and trusted my accountant. If I was thrown out of the game tomorrow I'd like to think that my family's future would be reasonably secure. I don't want Ashley and Natasha to have to struggle the way Sue and I did, that's a natural feeling for any father, but at the same time I can't help wondering whether Ashley's relatively privileged background will have made him hungry enough to make the grade in professional football. He'll have to make up his own mind and I won't be pushing him one way or the other but he's football crazy at the moment and of course I'll offer him every encouragement.

Some months ago, however, I got a first-hand taste of just how difficult Ashley is going to find it. His club side from around the corner in Formby were playing another boys' team from Kirkby – the tough Merseyside district that spawned Terry Mac and Phil Thompson. Ashley and his team-mates arrived at the ground with their strip washed and ironed, their boots polished and their designer tracksuits ready to combat the evening chill. The Kirkby boys on the other hand had holes in their ancient short-sleeved shirts, boots that looked like they'd never seen a brush or polish and the sort of commitment that turned the game into a war. The Kirkby team wanted to win and they did just that – convincingly. Ashley and his friends were sent back to their middle-class homes in Formby with their tails well and truly between their legs.

My mind went back to Irchester and my days as a schoolboy player and I clearly remembered the struggle to make it, every spare minute spent with the ball and football the passport out of poverty. For Ashley it's different, he's a child of the '80s with computers and radio-controlled toys, a snooker table and a bag of golf clubs. I'm not suggesting he should suffer to make progress, I am merely pointing out that he has far more choice than I ever did. At the end of the day I wonder whether Ashley, or hundreds of players like him, will have the sort of dogged determination it takes to go beyond schoolboy football and make it to the top.

I realise that I was probably more determined than most and although I despaired towards the end of my period with Northampton and seriously thought about quitting, I did have an in-built belief that I could make it. Sue, who admits she's not really interested in the game, was prepared to support me and Liverpool was the reward. I was an unknown quantity when we arrived on Merseyside and I was well aware of the fact that I had been signed for the squad rather than the team. Sue knew that too, and never tried to push us as a family, but nevertheless remembers that the wives' group – although cliquey – did extend the hand of friendship and made her feel welcome when she was a long way north of Northamptonshire and home.

There were flowers as a 'hello' present from one and the

offer of a babysitting service from another to give us a chance to take a look around the town. Sue has always made a point of being equally hospitable to subsequent newcomers. Footballers' wives have a hell of a lot to put up with and they are certainly not as 'green' as a lot of people think. Travelling as a squad is part of our job and the girls have built up their own support systems for dealing with the periods when we are away. Sue spends a bit of time with the wives of other players but over the years we have lived on Merseyside she has made a determined effort to develop a circle of friends who are in no way connected with the game. This suits me down to the ground because after you've spent a whole week with a bunch of lads, taking your fair share of the continuous stream of jibes and dressing-room jokes, it is nice to get away from football and relax properly.

Sue prides herself on her ability to spot a hanger-on at 50 paces so the sort of people who want to be a 'friend' of Phil Neal the footballer for the entertainment of their real friends in their local on a Sunday lunch-time are weeded out at a very early stage. What we've now established is a small group of people with whom we will stay close whether I remain famous or slip from the public eye at some future date. Nevertheless, there are still plenty of potholes when it comes to human nature and, despite all our best efforts, we have still been caught out a few times.

So-called businessmen like the one I mentioned earlier are easy to spot, more difficult are the people called in to do odd jobs. I swear we've got one of the most expensive bathroom suits on Merseyside simply because the contractor took a look at our house, made a note of my reputation and decided he could afford to up his price. We had a number of experiences like that and learned our lesson the hard way. Nowadays whenever we need any work done on the house I'm under strict orders to keep myself well out of the way and Sue reverts to her maiden name and handles all negotiations. It's a sad thing to report but I have to admit that we seem to have got a lot better value for money as a result.

People ask us a lot about the level of strain that exists within a football marriage and we have to admit that the potential for problems is always there. The long periods of separation pose one sort of problem while on the other hand the considerable amount of time we have on our hands compared with the average working people can cause a totally different form of strain. Fortunately, my career has been relatively injury-free so up until my final season with Liverpool, when I was on the point of leaving the club, I was involved to such an extent that I didn't ever have that feeling of time on my hands. As far as being away from home was concerned, Sue has always been very supportive, acknowledging that it was an important part of my job, and for my part I maintained regular contact with home and tried to do my best on the field to justify the separation.

No greater strain was placed on our marriage, however, than during the period between the Brussels massacre and Kenny's appointment as manager and my departure for Bolton in October 1985. Even during the early days at Northampton when we struggled to make ends meet life had its lighter moments and we always knew that things could only get better. With the realisation that my Anfield days were numbered a huge void appeared before me and for a long time I hadn't the first clue about how I was going to fill it. It was during this period that I became acutely conscious of the amount of time I had on my hands. Without a game to look forward to the daily grind of training became a chore rather than something I enjoyed and once it was out of the way the rest of the day stretched out before me and I didn't really care how I filled it.

For the first and, I sincerely hope, only time in my life I was in a state of depression and to my discredit I let it show. Sue had her own problems to contend with, having only recently left hospital, and having me around for most of the day should have been a help. As it turns out, all she can remember is that I was under her feet and 'hell to live with'. The children were feeling the strain, too. After years of being settled in the area and happy at their schools they were forced to face up to the possibility of a move that could take them hundreds of miles from Merseyside. Instead of encouraging them to see the positive side of the situation, I found myself snapping at them.

Then, in August, our family misery was complete when Sue's 27-year-old brother collapsed and died while playing cricket for his village team in Northamptonshire. We were devastated. I travelled down for the inquest and to help the family with all the arrangements and this was a tragedy guaranteed to take my mind off my own problems. Looking back, I think it probably brought me to my senses because I began to realise that whatever happened to me in the months ahead it could never have as appalling an impact on the family as my brother-in-law's untimely death. I think I pulled myself together overnight because if ever my support was needed it was then. And suddenly, without me feeling I had done anything to influence events, things began to move again.

The early round of managerial casualties offered the first openings and a few people began to approach me. Suddenly I began to feel wanted again, and when the Bolton job became vacant I had no hesitation in taking it. In all honesty it was a surprise to me that things happened so quickly in the end because in my more determined state of mind I had resigned myself to the possibility of remaining with Liverpool at least until the turn of the year. Becoming a manager presented a whole new set of problems to test the longevity and strength of our marriage but fortunately these were stresses of a positive kind and ones that the humour in our relationship was easily able to take care of.

Within weeks Sue was back to complaining that she never saw me and that when she did all I ever wanted to do was lie on the sofa and go to sleep. The children began to moan that I never took them out any more and bikes with punctured tyres began cluttering up the garage. Eventually, about six weeks into the job, I faced a three-pronged breakfast-time deputation: 'Give us a bit of your time or you'll be in trouble.'! The family had brought me to heel and that evening I took them all out for a meal to celebrate. The following weekend the bikes were mended and the garden was tidied and then I sat down and worked out some sort of timetable that would cope equally with the demands of getting Bolton Wanderers back on their feet and keeping the family happy.

Sue is the first to admit that like all couples we have had our ups and downs and that there have been times when she could cheerfully have throttled me. There have been times too when she wished that I could have been just an ordinary bloke with a good but regular job that didn't make such demands on my life and turn me into a public property. On the other hand, like me, she only has to look around her at our family, our home and our possessions to see what we have achieved. We live the life we lead today thanks to three things: football; Bob Paisley's wisdom in signing me at the right time; and our own level-headedness in making sure that we put something away for when the playing has to stop.

Sue boasts that she never goes into anything lightly and even though we were so young when we married she says she had thought things through and knew that she was making a commitment for life. The good times are relatively easy to cope with and fortunately we can't say we've had a lot of bad times, but there have been the odd one or two hiccups and I'm sure there are more to come. When they do it will be this determination and single-mindedness that will help steer us through them.

12

Bolton – The Way Forward

'Sleeping giant', said the man from Bolton the first time he phoned me, but it was only when I walked through those oak double doors at Burnden Park and took my seat in the manager's office that I realised this particular colossus would take one hell of a lot of waking!

'Go-ahead board', he promised, but I soon realised that I would have no money to spend on players.

'Great bunch of lads – just lacking the right motivation', he added. Instead I found myself saddled with a bunch of third-rate players living like fat cats on close to First Division wages, and all thanks to the generosity of my predecessors.

But despite all that, the Bolton Wanderers directors had something unique going for them – they wanted me! Their once-famous club was struggling at the bottom of Division Three and in danger of plumbing new depths for the first time in its history. Their managers had failed them, their players had let them down and they wanted me to sort things out. The Bolton directors were offering me a challenge and it was music to my ears. At Liverpool I felt I had suddenly become the forgotten man – a spent force – here I could be a saviour! At Burnden Park I could only do better than those that had gone before me and if everything went according to plan I had the opportunity to build a new career as a successful club manager.

I had none of the doubts that I had felt a few weeks earlier when I was considering the prospect of a move to

Grimsby Town. This was no east coast backwater, it was a football town in the true sense of the word. There isn't a football fan in the country who hasn't heard of Bolton Wanderers and Nat Lofthouse, the 'Lion of Vienna'. Four years earlier the club had been in the First Division and I had no doubts that they belonged there. I was anxious to play my part to ensure that they should return there as quickly as possible.

I remembered the words of a friend of mine, spoken during the final weeks of my career at Anfield. I had confessed my managerial ambitions and was discussing the offer from Grimsby and my doubts about accepting it. He told me: 'You've achieved a great deal in the game, kept your nose clean and earned a lot of respect. Football owes you a chance as a manager, but only one. There'll probably be a number of offers but it's up to you to make the right choice'. It wasn't until the Bolton offer came along that I fully understood what he meant. At Grimsby I was being offered a successful and established Second Division club while at Bolton there was a struggling Third Division side with a tremendous past, very little going for it at present and a future that lay in the lap of the gods. Yet, in the final analysis, there was no comparison.

Grimsby had done remarkably well to reach their current position and their previous manager had resigned – swapping the attractions of England's so-called 'bracing' east coast for the sunshine of the Canaries – because he felt he had taken the club to the very limit of its potential and I was inclined to agree with him. There was no real history or tradition associated with the club and it was hard to see how supporters could be attracted in significantly greater numbers to such an isolated outpost, even if the team did defy the odds and make it into the First Division. I feared Grimsby would end up like another Northampton Town or Carlisle United – a fairytale climb to the dizzy heights and then a fall that would be all more difficult to cope with, once success had been tasted.

Bolton, on the other hand, had been there before and I felt the directors and the fans remembered the taste of success and were hungry for a second helping. Burnden Park looked in urgent need of some cosmetic surgery, but as a stadium it had presence and it was easy to imagine it full again if there was a side on the field worth supporting. I was looking for a challenge and this was one I felt confident I could handle. 'You're on!' I told the man from Bolton. 'When shall I start?'.

I signed a two-and-a-half-year contract – the minimum period in which I felt I could realistically turn the club around. That gave me the rest of the 1985-86 season to save them from relegation to the Fourth Division and then two full seasons in which to build a new side capable of taking the club back to the Division One. In theory the projected time-scale appeared feasible, but in practice I was under no illusions about the amount of work that lay ahead of me. The directors also made a pledge: to get the club back into the black so that money could be made available to strengthen the team. Right from the start I left them with no doubts that cash will have to be made available if we are to significantly strengthen the team. For their part they warned me that assets would need to be liquidated to achieve this aim.

Together we have paid the price for the bad management of others, but once the re-financing of the club is complete I'm convinced that Bolton Wanderers will be a slimmed-down yet much fitter club, properly geared up to cope with the economic realities of professional football in the 1990s. Hauling the club back from the brink of financial disaster has naturally not been an entirely painless operation. Firstly, the directors were forced to sell the club's first-class training pitch at Bromwich Street, a facility that was so good that the Brazilian World Cup squad chose it from a long list of possible venues as their training camp in 1966.

The loss of Bromwich Street for housing development

was a bitter blow because alternative first-class training facilities in and around Bolton have been hard to find. The winter of 1985-86 turned out to be particularly wet in the north-west and I often wondered, as I watched the players trudging through ankle-deep mud on a local school field or at the nearby greyhound stadium, whether they'd have the strength to tie up their boots never mind play a full 90 minutes come Saturday afternoon. To be fair, there is a gym at Burnden Park but I have always been loath to make the players work inside too often. There is a limit to what you can do in the gym and as preparation for a game of football I feel the environment is totally false. Still, at the end of the day the sale of the training ground did bring the club a step nearer the black and the day when I can have money to spend on new players.

You cannot get away from the fact that the excesses of some of my predecessors must have contributed to the club's dire financial plight. For instance, when I took over there were 20 professionals on the books and 15 youngsters employed under the Government's YTS scheme. The wage structure in no way reflected the contribution that certain players were making to the team effort. A young first team regular who had risen through the ranks to establish himself could be picking up as little as £80 a week while a senior pro, well past his best and probably picked up from his previous club on a free transfer, was on a two-year contract at a basic wage of around £300 a week with a substantial bonus package on top of that.

I knew from the very beginning that a number of these senior players would not figure in my rebuilding plans and made it clear to other managers that I was prepared to let them go. The lack of response merely confirmed my own belief that, by Third Division standards, Bolton had saddled themselves with some pretty expensive liabilities. Take the youngsters, too. What an abuse of the YTS scheme! Because the Government was picking up the tab instead of the club, some people saw the scheme as an opportunity to sign up a string of promising schoolboys without having to worry too much either about the wage bill or the lad's potential to make the grade.

The club's youth team coach, Steve Carroll, with whom I was impressed and whom I kept on after I took over, had the thankless task of looking after these kids along with any of the other players who had drifted out of the first team pool, and he was quick to complain about the situation. His argument was that he had too many players to work with and too little time to devote to the specific needs of individual players. At the end of the day too many of these teenagers just didn't show enough promise to be offered terms, and with the people who had signed them in the first place long gone from the club it was left to me in the final week of the 1985-86 season to tell them that they had no future with Bolton Wanderers.

Many of these lads should never have been signed in the first place, others might have made it if they had been part of a smaller group and had been given the opportunity to benefit from the specialist coaching that a professional club can offer, but finally they remained just faces in the crowd until one afternoon in April, when I was forced to call them into my office one by one to tell them that their services would no longer be required by Bolton Wanderers once the season was over. That afternoon was just about the hardest I've faced since taking the job on, sitting behind my desk and facing these youngsters and remembering how I'd been in their shoes all those years ago at Northampton. The difference was that I had been one of only a handful of apprentices and Ron Flowers, Bill Baxter and Dave Bowen had all known exactly who I was and the extent of my potential.

Now, as manager, I knew the club could not afford their wages and that Steve – or any coach for that matter – could not be expected to work with so many players. Some of the youngsters put on a brave face, others seemed close to tears at the prospect of their dreams being shattered so quickly and at the idea of having to face up to a future away from the full-time game. I tried to offer a small crumb of comfort to each of the lads as they shuffled into my office. I told them that I was only human and that it was possible I had made a mistake. I urged them to use the remaining weeks of the season to try to find a new club and promised that Bolton would do everything in its power to help them.

The reality, though, was that most of the youngsters would either drift out of the game completely – disillusioned by their failure to make the grade – or find themselves a club competing at a reasonable level in amateur football in the hope that they might attract the attention of a league scout at a later stage. Naturally I'd seen scores of young hopefuls turned away from Anfield at the end of their apprenticeships, but somehow things didn't seem to be so bad for them. It's well known in football that the Third and Fourth Division clubs often keep a close eye on the apprentices at Liverpool, Everton or Manchester United, and when a youngster is released they move in and offer him terms. They reason that if a big club had confidence in him in the first place then he must be able to play if not necessarily at the highest level. Release a lad from Bolton, though, and you'll find very few takers. Of the young players I let go at the end of the season, only one managed to get fixed up with a Football League club, Stockport County.

For the rest, the way ahead in football will be very tough. Most will find the physical demands of top-flight non-league football too great and only the really determined boys will survive and keep alive their hopes of finally making it back into the big-time, perhaps a couple of seasons from now. Sadly, most of the others, if they don't drift out of the game altogether, will finish up playing their football on a Saturday afternoon or Sunday morning as the star of their local pub side.

From the moment I decided that football management was for me I began looking around for a potential number two. I wanted someone of like mind so that could only mean a former player with experience of the Anfield set-up, because I knew that the basis of my managerial philosophy would always be Liverpool Football Club. I talked to a number of people and had several options, but in the end I chose Colin Irwin, and it genuinely surprised me when the reaction of a number of people in the game was: 'Colin who?'.

Colin is a straight-talking 'Scouser' with a passion for football but his career failed to peak at the level that it should have done because he was at Anfield at a time when Phil Thompson and Alan Hansen were consistently on top form. Eventually, with just 29 first team appearances to his name, he decided that he should pursue his career away from Anfield. A fine example of Colin's reputation within the game is the fact that John Toshack wanted him at Vetch Field and was prepared to invest £340,000 – still Swansea City's record transfer fee. Sadly, though, Colin wasn't around long enough to fulfil his potential there either because after just 49 first team appearances, his career was cut cruelly short by a knee injury and he was forced to retire from the game in 1983.

We hadn't been particularly close at Liverpool, but we shared a keen commitment to training and I knew that Colin's attitude to the game was broadly in line with mine. I met up with him by chance shortly after he arrived back on Merseyside after coaching in Australia, and when he told me he was looking for an opening in the game I told him that I was planning to try my hand at management and promised to keep him in mind when the time came.

I suppose football is no different from any other walk of life, really. So much can happen because of who you know rather than what you know. Colin was a trusted team-mate on the lookout for a job and he bumped into me just at the right time. I'd thought about other former colleagues, among them David Johnson, but in the end there was something about Colin's attitude that made me feel he was ideal. I think it might have had something to do with the way his playing career had collapsed so tragically. Being forced to retire so prematurely had come as a tremendous blow to him but he had still retained his passion for the game and was anxious to remain a part of it. I feel I've given him the opportunity to achieve something in football and although the trainer's dugout can never provide the feeling of actually being out there on the field, it is still a whole lot closer to the action than a seat in the stand.

Football seems to be a drug to some people, particularly those who have been involved in the game at a professional level. It doesn't seem to matter how many knocks they have taken or how many times a board has turfed them out on their ear, they still keep coming back for more. Since I've been at Bolton I have regularly been surprised by some of the names at the bottom of the steady stream of letters I've received asking for work. Some of them have enjoyed successful managerial careers in recent years but have fallen out with their clubs for one reason or another, others appear to have suffered appallingly at the hands of disgruntled fans or directors, but still they come back wanting more. Somehow I don't think I would be one of them if things turned sour on me.

Naturally, I consider myself more fortunate than most because my ten years at Anfield and my testimonial season have, as long as I'm reasonably careful, made me financially secure. I'm staying in football because I want to and not because I need the money, and I'm hoping that this will keep the pressure off me and make me a better manager. If I fail – and believe me I will be the first to know – I will slip quietly away from the game and pursue a totally different career. Of course I hope and believe that this won't happen – all I'm saying is that I won't be a glutton for further punishment in the event that it does.

Sadly for the old school of managers, the face of the modern game is changing and all clubs are operating to the tightest of budgets and saving money wherever and whenever they can. Gone are the days of the huge playing staffs and gone, too, are the big back-room teams. Many clubs are coming round to the idea of player-managers, particularly in the Third and Fourth Divisions, and now that Kenny Dalglish has proved that the two jobs can be successfully combined even at the highest level, I'm sure many more clubs are likely to follow suit. This is bad news then for the army of established but older managers who are finding jobs harder and harder to come by. Some of them must face up to the unhappy prospect of never working in the game again.

It's not just the managers who are suffering. Many clubs are being forced to cut back on their scouting networks as well. At Bolton our back-room team on the playing side numbers four; Colin and myself, Steve to look after the young players and Peter Nightingale, the physiotherapist. Like many other clubs we operate at a minimum staffing level and that means a lot of work to share out among us. Besides looking after our three teams, we are increasingly forced to travel the country watching future opponents because we cannot afford to buy in reports from experts outside the area, and then there's the need to watch potential signings in action so that we can assess their suitability for Bolton Wanderers. It's a punishing schedule and it took a lot of getting used to in the first few weeks. I felt the workload was tough enough just for a manager but to combine those responsibilities with my obligations as a player pushed things to the very limit.

In my first five weeks at Burnden Park I managed just one day off – a Thursday after a mid-week game – and, with the kids at school, I decided to whisk Sue off to a favourite restaurant just around the corner from our home. We'd just sat down to our meal when in walked Mick Lyons, a friend and former Merseyside rival in his days with Everton. Mick had accepted the job I'd turned down at Grimsby and was apparently feeling the strain every bit as much as I was. He claimed it was his first day off, too, and instead of taking the chance to catch up on family gossip, Sue found herself eavesdropping on an hour of football talk as Mick and I swapped stories about the pressure of football management. As punishment I spent the rest of that precious day off painting the spare bedroom!

Seriously, though, I soon began to appreciate why Kenny Dalglish left himself out of the Liverpool team so much during the early part of the 1985-86 season, because I found myself doing the same. Then as we both began to get to grips with the demands of management the playing side of the job also started to fit in. I've decided to continue playing in the 1986-87 season and because I take this aspect of my job so seriously I have been forced to lay down some ground rules for myself. In my view it is too easy to believe that you have to do everything connected with the management of the club yourself – if I did that then I would never have enough energy left to make a contribution to the team – so I delegate responsibility wherever I feel able to do so. Colin takes responsibility for the daily training routine and seems to have established the right level of rapport with the players. Even the senior pros seem to respect his methods and his honesty.

We both share the Liverpool idea that players should be treated as adults and not as kids that just happen to be able to perform with a ball. I would never dream of fining a player for his misdemeanours, partly because I feel it is a particularly degrading practice that would be laughed out of any conventional workplace, but primarily because I'm aiming to surround myself with players who will be proud to wear the white shirt of Bolton Wanderers and share in the feeling of satisfaction that will surround a successful return to the top flight. If a player steps out of line at Burnden Park, he's dragged in for extra training – I believe we should punish his lungs rather than his family's pocket. This could be a throwback to my one and only brush with the fines system back at Northampton, but regardless of its origins I do believe most vehemently that it is the best policy.

It is almost a year now since I first walked into Burnden Park and I think I have already made enough changes to ensure that my own personality and attitude to the game have been stamped on the club, but looking back to that first day I remember being staggered by the shambles that lay before me. Charlie Wright, my predecessor, enjoyed a long and successful career as a goalkeeper and went on to manage York City before he drifted out of the game and into the licensed trade. Like a number of other goalkeepers, though, his services as a specialist coach were at a premium and he began looking after Bolton's goalkeepers some time before John McGovern became manager. Charlie was apparently working a couple of afternoons a week at the club when the new manager took over. The pair of them soon hit it off and Charlie was elevated first to youth team coach and then to first team coach – in effect he became McGovern's right-hand man.

The club was already on the downward spiral, both financially and on the field of play – although I'm sure John McGovern would argue that the latter stemmed directly from the former, and the fact that he was forced to sell the very players who would otherwise have formed the nucleus of his rebuilding programme seems to support this argument. However when the going got tough, the two of them apparently fell out because when John – Bolton having slipped into the Third Division – finally lost his job, Charlie was more than willing to stay on as caretaker manager. Like others before him, he got a few good results, and like other directors before them, the Bolton board soon confirmed him as the club's permanent boss and that's when my problems started.

Charlie Wright had no money to spend on transfers so he set about rebuilding the team around experienced players who were coming to the end of their careers. He offered an attractive contract to Asa Hartford – an idol with West

Bromwich Albion and Manchester City, but already on the way out with Norwich. Then, even more surprisingly, he offered terms to Sam Allardyce. Sam was a former Bolton player who'd left for pastures new some seasons before but had never really established himself anywhere. He was down and out at Huddersfield Town when Charlie pounced and to Sam the offer must have seemed like Christmas. He was given a long contract and a basic wage that would have attracted some First Division players. Sam couldn't sign quickly enough and I couldn't blame him.

You couldn't wish to meet a nicer bloke than Sam Allardyce, he's a good honest workhorse but he's never been more than an average player. When I took over at Burnden Park he didn't have a chance. Thanks to Charlie Wright's outrageous view of Sam's worth, the lad was an overpaid luxury that I just couldn't afford to keep whether I wanted to or not. To be fair I think Sam knew as much himself because on day one he was the first player to come knocking at the manager's door. 'Boss, I want to know my future here', he said.

I'd only been in the job a couple of hours, so what was I supposed to say? My mind flashed back to a classic occasion at Liverpool when Brian Kettle, skipper of the 'Red's' Central League side for as many years as anyone could remember but never ever in the first team decided it was time for a showdown with Bob Paisley. The meeting was fixed and Brian steamed in with the question: 'Have I got a future at Anfield, Boss?'. Bob knew what was coming and was ready with the answer: 'Come on, Brian, what do'ya think I am: a fortune teller?'. It was the end of the conversation and Brian was back in the dressing-room before he fully appreciated what had happened.

I couldn't bring myself to be so smart with Sam even though I knew he didn't fit into my plans. It was my first taste of life as a manager and already I was beginning to realise just what I had let myself in for. No longer was I responsible only for the welfare of Phil Neal and family, I was 'Boss' to a bunch of experienced professional footballers and father-figure to a group of youngsters I had never met and – brutal though it may sound – might never have wanted! I was a thoughtful man that evening as I drove home to the Wirral.

I learned a great deal in my first few months as a Football League manager and soon realised that I could expect no favours from anyone and would survive only if I kept my wits about me and was suspicious of everyone. Managers who had been in the game for years were soon on the phone testing me out. Bob Stokoe at Carlisle wanted to off-load a player at a giveaway £5,000 but I knew he'd signed him on a free transfer only a few months earlier and he hadn't managed to force his way into the side. Then during a particularly harsh spell of weather the Stockport County manager got to hear that Ron Atkinson was letting Bolton use United's all-weather training facility at The Cliff. He was on the phone the next morning, suggesting we should arrange a practice match forgetting, I suppose, that we were due to meet the very next week in the Freight Rover Trophy. I enquired about a player at Lincoln City and was staggered by the asking price of £100,000. 'He's a good player and I'd like to hang on to him, but I have to agree that he's ready for a change of club', he told me over the phone. I'm not surprised the lad was ready for a change of club – he'd been at Sincil Bank for 11 years. But I was looking at a fraction of that fee and would never have paid the asking price even if we had had the money.

Then there was the case of Steve Kinsey, a promising youngster who had been with Manchester City since leaving school but, despite more than 50 appearances in the first team, had never established himself. City had sent Steve out on loan a couple of times already and I felt confident that their manager Billy McNeill would be happy to let the lad come to Bolton for a few weeks. Nothing could have been further from the truth, however, because McNeill huffed and puffed, avoided my phone calls and then, when I finally confronted him, told me that the player didn't think a loan move would be in the best interests of his career. Now I knew that was rubbish because a number of people who knew Steve and were aware of my interest in him had told me that he would be delighted to play for Bolton. I felt well and truly messed about.

Naturally, I respect Billy McNeill's right to handle the player in any way that he sees fit, but why couldn't he have been straight with me? As on so many other occasions in my career I was only ever looking for a straight answer, and as a result of his prevarication I spent a number of days hanging around in the belief that I had solved one of my short-term problems instead of looking for an alternative. Experienced managers may well be able to justify their reasons for some of the antics they get up to, but I hope that experience doesn't have quite the same effect on me. Of course, I'm as determined as the next man to drive a hard bargain, but honesty is equally important to me. In Billy McNeill's shoes I would have given a straight answer, either: 'Yes, the lad can join you' or 'No, he's central to my plans and I can't afford to let him out on loan'. Either answer would have been preferable to a string of half-promises and then, finally, nothing.

As with so many clubs, the crazy days of the late 1970s and early 1980s, when players could command astronomical wages and transfer fees were calculated in Monopoly money, hit Bolton Wanderers hard. The present board of directors and yours truly have inherited the legacy of those spendthrift days. Football is finally waking up to the fact that it cannot expect to lead a charmed life immune to the liquidator indefinitely. No club has gone out of business since Accrington Stanley, but last season saw a number teetering on the brink and I'm sure the day of reckoning will arrive for at least one of them in the near future. I have no wish to see Bolton Wanderers in that sort of predicament, so I welcome the sensible housekeeping of the present board of directors.

Successful sides have been built on tight budgets in the past – Bill Shankly's first Liverpool team and the Bobby Robson's Ipswich Town are classic examples – but in both cases the manager did know that in the right circumstances money could be found if a player who could provide a vital missing ingredient suddenly became available. This is all I have asked of the directors at Bolton.

To cope with this, and to keep the bank manager happy, they are negotiating the sale of part of the Burnden Park complex to the local council. This transaction will put the club back in credit, create a superb local authority sports complex at Burnden Park and, most importantly, provide some much needed cash for team-building.

There is only one problem from my point of view, and that stems from a deal that has apparently been struck with the council to lay an artificial surface at Burnden Park within the next couple of years to enable the pitch itself to be used as a municipal facility several nights a week. On one hand I'm all in favour of Burnden Park being made available to as many people as possible, but on the other – like so many other footballers – I'm not totally convinced that all-weather surfaces are good for the game. Indeed, Don Howe appears to share my view because I understand that his final flashpoint came after the Highbury chairman, Dennis Hill-Wood, tossed a coin at the end of an Arsenal-Luton Cup replay and agreed to stage the third game at Kenilworth Road rather than on a neutral ground. Howe felt the chairman had put his side at a disadvantage by agreeing to a second match on astroturf and I have to say that I would have shared his concern.

I realise that after the success of the Queens Park Rangers and Luton Town experiments, a number of clubs – particularly those whose grounds drain badly – are bound to be tempted by the idea of a surface which enables them always to play their fixtures on the appointed date. However, the artificial surface demands a totally different discipline from the conventional game and I'm afraid I don't believe it is in the true spirit of football. Call me old-fashioned if you like, but for me the game evolved on grass and should therefore stay on grass. When my opinion is sought in the boardroom that is the case I will argue.

That said, I know that I am working with a board of directors who, like me, have the best interests of the club at heart. My aim is to get Bolton Wanderers back into the First Division, and although I cannot realistically expect to achieve this within the duration of my present contract, I still hope to make substantial progress towards my goal. The directors of Bolton Wanderers want a successful and financially secure club, and I want my career as a manager to be as rewarding as my years as a player. Between us I believe we can give that hard core of supporters who have been forced to live on their memories for so long a new era of success to look forward to and a club that can rightly challenge its mighty neighbours, Manchester United and Manchester City.

13
Postscript

There's far more to football management than meets the eye, and although I didn't have any illusions about the enormity of the task facing me when I stepped into the manager's chair at Burnden Park, I was all the same surprised by the way my opinions were soon influenced by my new range of responsibilities. Over at Anfield, Kenny Dalglish was also coming to terms with responsibility and the pressure that inevitably accompanies it, although he did enjoy a great deal of support in the form of Bob Paisley, who assumed the role of a wise father figure during the months of transition. My job was to keep Bolton in the Third Division at all costs and, to be frank, things were looking pretty bleak when I arrived. Kenny's somewhat awesome task was to restore Liverpool's pride in the wake of the Heysel Stadium tragedy and take the club back to the top of the pile after the Merseyside humiliation of Everton's League Championship the previous season.

With no money to spend and no prospect of the situation changing in the foreseeable future, I spent my days scouring the lists of Third and Fourth Division players who were available either on loan or free transfer, but even when I saw one or two I fancied there was always the problem of how we could afford to pay their wages. Over at Anfield, with the full glare of the media directed on him, Kenny was restructuring his side. Alan Kennedy and I moved on and Kenny – controversially as far as the press were concerned – left himself out of the side, leaving no doubts as to his intention to follow the example of Bob Paisley after Bill Shankly in creating a new generation Liverpool. He played Jan Molby in a 'sweeper' role and this was a tactical ploy that many observers found difficult to understand. Jan had at first found it difficult to come to terms with the pace of the English game after his spell in Holland with Ajax and, although he had made a great effort to shed some surplus pounds during the close season, Brian Glanville in *The Sunday Times* was still moved to describe him as looking more like a Danish international darts player than a footballer after one game in the early part of the season.

The turning point for Jan came during the final weeks of my career at the club. Liverpool had been drawn at home against Manchester United in the Milk Cup and I was named as late substitute. United went off like an express train and were a goal up midway through the first half. Jan couldn't do anything right, he was being constantly caught in possession, looked sluggish moving forward and his distribution could have been bettered by an average player in a Sunday pub team. It looked odds-on to everyone that Kenny would have to take him off, but something inside me – even though it would have meant I would get a game – told me that the substitution would be wrong. At half-time the lads trudged off the field frustrated at their lack of progress and Jan's head was really down. I took him to one side in the dressing-room and told him in no uncertain terms that he had been brought to the club because he was supposedly a big-occasion player and reminded him that he would be unlikely to find a better stage on which to display his talents for some time to come. 'Get out there and show them what you can do,' I implored him.

In the second half he was a revelation, storming through the United defence to blast in an equaliser that had the massed ranks of the Kop parting in anticipation of the ball bursting the net, and then just minutes later, his confidence restored, he stepped up to slot home the penalty that gave us victory. I'm not trying to overplay my role in the transformation of Jan Molby, but at the same time I'm sure it was that game that proved the turning point for him. He went on to become an inspiration in the heart of the Liverpool team and I'm sure Kenny would be the first to admit that he had a great deal to do with the club's success last season.

At Bolton the stage couldn't have been more different. I'd done my dust in the lower divisions all those seasons ago, but it had been easy to forget just how tough they are. I picked myself in the centre of the defence for my first game against Doncaster, figuring that it would be as good a place as any to give the other players the once over. Ironically, Rovers also had a player-manager in their line-up that day, Dave Cusack, and I was looking forward to a natter with him after the game to find out how he was getting along. However, I soon discovered that Dave wasn't the sort you invite into your office for a post-match drink. He spent most of the game kicking me whenever he had the opportunity and then towards the end of the match, with Bolton in firm control, he brought me down once too often and when I leapt to my feet to complain he spat in my face! Welcome to the real world, I thought, as I walked down the tunnel at the final whistle.

Slowly but surely, Kenny began to make progress at Anfield. His restructured side began to string some results together and after a few months of the season they were in the pack and chasing the runaway leaders Manchester United. Likewise at Burnden Park I was settling into my new role and, although there were still the odd moments of despair, we weren't losing as often as we could have done and the fear that I had seen in the eyes of some of the lads when I first took over was beginning to be replaced with something approaching confidence.

One of the first problems I encountered with the players was their total lack of belief in themselves when it came to away matches. As far as they were concerned, these couldn't be won no matter how hard they tried, and even at home their heads dropped from the moment they went a goal down. They needed a psychiatrist as much as they needed a new manager, and Colin and I had to set about a programme of re-education. At Liverpool confidence had never been a problem. Even when the results were bad the team still had a total belief in itself. For the Anfield players going a goal down merely inspired them to even greater heights and it is often argued that the side is at its most deadly when a goal behind. I knew Kenny wouldn't be sharing my problems in that area!

One headache we did share, though, was goalkeepers. Bruce Grobbelaar was as frustrating as ever – brilliant one minute, throwing a soft goal in the next – and at Bolton I inherited a 'keeper who was going through one of the darkest phases of his career. It was clear from the word go that a new goalkeeper was a priority if I was to plug the leaking defence and I began looking around for a replacement. Understandably, the news filtered through to the press and before I knew where I was the lad was knocking on my door for an explanation. His timing was about as good as his handling – he chose to come calling the morning after a night match in which his mistakes had cost us two goals and three important points. I told him there was no use in my denying that I was looking for a replacement for him and gave him my reasons there and then. Incredibly, he countered by telling me that it was the newspaper speculation about his future that had ruined his confidence. I couldn't believe what I was hearing because in my experience the one thing guaranteed to make a player raise his game is the news that the manager is thinking of replacing him.

Liverpool really got their act together in the last third of the season and began to look serious title contenders. At Bolton we were at last beginning to take positive steps towards our own goal of Third Division survival. The two clubs, and Kenny and I as managers, were poles apart in the playing sense but in our respective backyards we were both beginning to get a sniff of achievement.

Kenny's success with the League and Cup double has earned him a place in the record books and he deserves high praise. I was up there among the doubters in the beginning and I'm still not sure about the long term, but the man has already achieved something that neither Mr Shankly nor Bob Paisley were able to do and it is a testimony to his single-mindedness. He kept faith with his tactics when his critics were calling for change, he left himself out of the side even though the early season results were a clear indication that he should be playing and then, in the last third of the season when the pressure was on, he slotted himself back into the side and scored some vital goals, among them the Championship decider at Chelsea. Add to that the League and Cup double and then throw in the fact that he collected a record number of Scottish caps and went on to pick up the Freedom of the City of Glasgow, and you have to admit that 1986 turned out to be a pretty successful year for him.

By comparison, my achievements have been modest, although my 14 appearances in a Liverpool shirt did earn me yet another League Championship medal. However, I did get the satisfaction of another visit to Wembley when Bolton made it to the final of the Freight Rover Trophy. Although on the day we were second best and went down 3-0, the occasion was the real winner. A crowd of 54,500 watched the match and it was a real family day out without the slightest hint of trouble. My mind flashed back to the very same week a year earlier and football's night of shame – the contrast couldn't have been more stark.

Back in Bolton we were treated like winners by the people of the town and I could see from the faces of many of the players that it was something they weren't very used to. The local council laid on a civic reception and everyone enjoyed themselves. However, standing there in the middle of it all, I knew I had just one more job to do that season and it was a job I was not looking forward to at all. My season drew to a close in much the same way as it began way back in August 1985 – with a meeting. This time, though, instead of Phil Neal the player knocking on the door of John Smith the chairman, it was Graham Bell the player meeting Phil Neal the manager.

Graham, who is 31 and has recently become a father, doesn't fit into my plans for 1986-87. A number of other players were also released, but knew about their fate ahead of that last game at Wembley. Graham was different. I had figured I might need him in the match and so delayed breaking the news until afterwards – cynical maybe, but the good of the club has to come first. Telling him that he was a free agent and acknowledging that he might find it very difficult to get fixed up with another League club was the hardest thing I had to do in my first season as the manager of Bolton Wanderers. Naturally the lad was heartbroken and felt let down. An image of Mr Smith flashed through my mind as I faced Graham on the other side of my desk. I didn't feel good about what I was doing, but my conscience was clear because I was speaking the truth and looking him in the eye!

In exactly twelve months my career had been transformed. A year ago I had led Liverpool in Brussels on football's night of shame, that afternoon at Burnden Park I was facing up to my responsibilities as a football manager. There was compassion on the one hand for the unfortunate player, but on the other I had already learned the hard way that in this game success and sentiment can never mix.

Honours

Football League: Div. One: A record number of 16 League titles
Div. Two: Four titles

European Cup: Winners – 1976-77, 1977-78, 1980-81, 1983-84.

UEFA Cup: Winners – 1972-73, 1975-76.

FA Cup: Winners – 1965, 1974, 1986.

Football League Cup: Winners – 1981, 1982, 1983, 1984.

In season 1985-86, Kenny Dalglish in his first season as player-manager steered Liverpool to a Football League and FA Cup Double. Phil Neal, by virtue of his appearances in the side at the start of the season qualified for his seventh League Championship medal.

Liverpool F.C. – the record

Founded: 1892
Post War Managers: George Kay, Don Welsh, Phil Taylor, Bill Shankly, Bob Paisley, Joe Fagan, Kenny Dalglish.
Most League Appearances: Ian Callaghan (640) 1960-78
Most Capped Player: Emlyn Hughes (59) England
Record Transfer Fee Received: £500,000 from SV Hamburg for Kevin Keegan in June 1977
Highest Transfer Fee Paid: £900,000 to Brighton & Hove Albion for Mark Lawrenson in August 1981

Index